T0109228

The Perception Myth

The Perception Myth

A Guide to Challenging Your
Personal Myths and Discovering
Your Inner Greatness

By Brad Wheelis

Skyhorse Publishing

Skyhorse Publishing books may be purchased in bulk at special discounts for sales promotion, corporate gifts, fund-raising, or educational purposes. Special editions can also be created to specifications. For details, contact the Special Sales Department, Skyhorse Publishing, 307 West 36th Street, 11th Floor, New York, NY 10018 or info@skyhorsepublishing.com.

Skyhorse® and Skyhorse Publishing® are registered trademarks of Skyhorse Publishing, Inc.®, a Delaware corporation.

Visit our website at www.skyhorsepublishing.com.

10 9 8 7 6 5 4 3 2 1

Library of Congress Cataloging-in-Publication Data is available on file.

Cover design by Welly Santoso
Cover photo credit ROF Industries Inc.

ISBN: 978-1-62914-648-5
Ebook ISBN: 978-1-63220-086-0

Printed in the United States of America

Contents

Prologue

WHO IS BRAD?

It was the week before Christmas, and our little Dodge Dart Swinger was chugging wearily up Tennessee's Great Smoky Mountains. We had just spent the last three years in the Republic of Panama and were heading to my father's new military assignment. The plan was to stop in St. Louis to visit my grandparents before pressing on to Oklahoma, where we would settle for the next three years. But the old family car had other plans.

As we meandered through the picturesque country, Dad realized something was amiss. The rear end was going out on the car, and we could hear ominous grinding. We all knew it wouldn't be long before the car gave out completely.

Just in time, we pulled into a small town where Dad managed to locate a mechanic who said he could make the necessary repairs. One of the mechanic's assistants drove us to the nearest motel, where we could watch the town's holiday parade go by while waiting for the car to be fixed.

It was bitterly cold, and the mechanic's assistant was driving a pickup. My mom and sister jumped up front. I hopped in the back and shivered for the three blocks it took to reach the motel. My sister Amy was a worrywart and fought back tears all the way. But I was resigned to our mishap. This was part of life, our life as have-nots.

Growing up in a military family provided a front row seat to the class system. At the top of the social ladder were the commissioned officers—the "haves"—while the non-commissioned officers (NCOs)—the "have-nots"—hovered down below. The grown-ups didn't mingle across the classes and neither did the kids for the most part. That's just the way it was.

That was my perception of our family. My father was a non-commissioned officer in the military and did not make a lot of money. We never went without the necessities, but there were few luxuries. While my friends wore IZOD and Docksiders, I wore Le Tigre and off-brand shoes.

Not surprisingly, when our car broke down, it also happened that we were flat broke. Mom and Dad had to call my aunt to wire some money for the car repairs, promising to pay her back. They always did. My aunt had married into money, and we all envied her lifestyle. She made regular trips to Las Vegas, bought expensive clothes without batting an eye, and drove luxury cars. One day, I thought, I would be as rich as Aunt Annabelle.

After a few hours, the mechanic brought us our car, and we resumed our journey to St. Louis. Every few miles, Dad turned down the radio to listen to the car and make sure it wasn't making any strange noises. We arrived at my grandparents' house without further ado and enjoyed our first reunion in years. But all too soon we were off again, en route to Altus, Oklahoma, where a new home and new school awaited us.

Boy, did I hate school! As a shy kid, it was tough to fit in. And I was also deeply embarrassed about the way I looked. I was a geeky kid and wore glasses that made me look like something from outer space. Having the perception that our family wasn't good enough didn't help matters either. We knew our place—at least I did. In my view, I didn't measure up because I came from an average family, not one that was well-to-do. And to me that meant everything.

I was very aware of the social differences. I often caught myself wishing that I were the son of an officer. Then I would be one of the "haves." I would be privileged. I would be respected. Respect meant everything to me. It meant you were somebody; you mattered; you counted. But I couldn't feel any of that as the son of an NCO. Instead, I felt wildly inadequate and yearned for something better.

My feelings didn't revolve only around my family's social status. Something more traumatic contributed to my strong emotions of inadequacy.

Early in life, I had suffered from severe physical issues that left me with an appalling body image. When my mother was pregnant with me, she had contracted measles. Luckily I escaped without any major birth defects that could have left me brain damaged. But I was left with terrible eyesight. Before the age of ten, I'd had to battle through several operations on my eyes. They led to a dreadful fear of hospitals. And after my last eye surgery, I vowed never to undergo another operation in my life.

Hospitals were very frightening to me. Every time the anesthetist put the mask over my face, I became terrified. It was cold, everybody was hidden behind face masks, and my mother, the only person who could have comforted me, was not allowed to be by my side in the operating room.

For years, my life consisted of an endless regime of operations on my eyes that did little to improve my sight. I was forced to wear ugly, round eyeglasses that looked like Coke bottles. I loathed them with a consuming passion. And they became the symbol for everything that was wrong in my life.

It's hard to exhibit self-esteem and take the initiative to meet new friends when you've got four eyes. At least, I felt like I had four eyes. When I was a kid, glasses were not commonplace. Big, thick lenses stood out and looked bizarre. I constantly heard the "four eyes" taunt from my peers. I knew it came with the territory. I was destined to be made fun of and I bravely shouldered the lumps. But that didn't assuage my hurt. Ironic to think that, years later, glasses would actually become fashionable. Who knew? Maybe if I'd known that back then, I might have felt less of an outsider.

But another physical abnormality disturbed me even more than my eyesight. I have an unusual condition called pectus excavatum. That's Latin for a concave chest. If I lie on my back, you can use my chest as a serving dish. I often do when I'm at home alone watching a movie. It's the perfect place to store my popcorn.

I might joke about it now, but it was no laughing matter when I was a kid. I felt paralyzed by this awful-looking chest and thought of myself as a freak. You wouldn't believe the lengths to which I went to hide this from others. I'd rarely be seen bare chested. And if I went to a swimming pool, I would keep my shirt on until I reached the edge of the pool, then whip it off quickly and plunge into the water.

The kids who saw my chest were quick to point out that it was "different." And in my mind, "different" was definitely not good. I remember one horrendous day in gym class when a classmate said to me, "It looks like a bowling ball hit your chest."

My stomach lurched and I felt like bursting into tears. Somehow I kept my composure and laughed along with the others. He never brought it up again. But that comment haunted me every day for years.

Thoughts of my chest dominated my mind continually. On my morning walks, I worried the wind would blow my shirt into the concave chest, causing me more embarrassment. If only I could have had a moment's rest away from the damned chest.

I guess in retrospect there were a few respites, although it didn't seem like it at the time. One escape was through my imagination. I was an avid car enthusiast, even as a child. I built myself a pretty good Matchbox car collection and erected a LEGO city on a sheet of plywood in my bedroom. I would drive LEGO cars around the city for hours. My imagination allowed me to be whomever I wanted and ran rampant. I could drive one of the fancy cars in my collection and pretend to be somebody important and famous. It was my escape, and I spent countless hours playing by myself, letting my mind wander into another world where I was unjudged.

The car collection offered me all the riches of the universe. It was exactly what I craved. And for a while, as I lost myself in my make-believe world, I could cease to think about my deformed chest.

Yes indeed, life was good when I was alone with my cars. But outside of the bedroom, I felt like a freak. Why was it so impossible to be normal? Why couldn't I be like the other kids? These were questions I asked myself constantly, all the while wishing for some magic wand that would change my physical shell.

My self-perceived inadequacies and low self-esteem were exacerbated by insensitive comments and probing questions from my schoolmates. They were never satisfied, and the curiosity was unending. Throughout my teenage years, I never dated—I was too afraid of rejection. After all, I reasoned, who would want someone with such a horrible handicap? A shy introvert, I became a classic loner, capable of making only a friend or two on each military base where we lived. And it was hard moving every three years and trying to establish new friendships.

My parents tried to make it fun and exciting. When they received new orders to move, they would gather us around and my mom would show us the area on a map, filling our ears with masses of information about the new location. It was like a new world. And she made it sound each time as though we were being given a fresh start at the new base.

A fresh start was exactly what I wanted to hear. Having not made many friends at the current base, now I had a new opportunity to make some at the next. I told myself things would be different this time. I vowed to be more outgoing, but rarely mustered the courage to strike up conversation with the kids in the new school.

There was one move, though, when I made a drastic change. For years, my family called me by my initials—B.J.—short for Bradley Joseph. As I got older, my classmates taught me that those initials also stood for something of a sexual nature. By the time we moved to Knob Noster, Missouri, in 1978, I had made the decision that from then on I would be known as Brad—dropping the B.J. and all that it intimated forever. The new kids never knew about my earlier nickname. And for me, it was the first realization that I could change things in my life. I had the power to do it. All I needed was the will and the belief.

Easier said than done. I didn't use my newfound power much after that. It turned out to be much easier to change one's name than to change one's personality. The shy kid hung around for years.

Throughout those tough and emotionally painful adolescent years, I dreamed about my future. I was going to make good money and be hugely successful. Most importantly, people would respect me.

I remember one day in Panama when I told my mother I wanted to earn fifty thousand dollars a year by the time I was thirty. She chuckled and said that was a good goal for a kid to have. Back then, it was a monstrous amount of money, the same as a six-figure salary today. It was that kind of daydreaming that got me through those awful teenage years. I knew better times had to be ahead and somehow I would make my dreams come true.

> I could change things in my life. I had the power to do it. All I needed was the will and the belief.

And then Jessica Savitch entered my life. Jessica was an anchor for NBC News. While living in Panama, I would watch her weekend broadcasts to learn what was going on stateside. Jessica was mesmerizing and had that rare ability to make you feel she was speaking directly to you. She was poised, beautiful, and charming. In other words, she was perfect. And how I wished I could be perfect like Jessica.

When my English teacher declared our next book review would be a biography, I chose Jessica Savitch's *Anchorwoman*. Until then, I'd never read a book in its entirety. I didn't care for books much. They were difficult to read with my poor eyesight.

But this book was different. There was a real person behind it, someone I could relate to on so many levels, both emotionally and physically. As a child, she had felt awkward and eventually found solace in high school working for a local radio station. In her book, Jessica explained about being an outcast and not quite fitting in with her classmates. It seemed as though she had found the answer—

become a famous broadcaster and life becomes perfect. Or, at least, that's what I derived from her book.

Suddenly I felt as if a bolt of lightning had struck me. And then I knew. I just *knew*! Then and there I declared I was going to be a broadcaster. And I was very serious. Armed with a microphone and tape recorder, I conducted mock newscasts and tried my hand at being a DJ. I loved it.

Then the most awful news came. I woke up for school on October 24, 1983, turned on the television, and heard that Jessica Savitch had died in a horrible car accident. I was devastated. Heartbroken doesn't begin to describe the way I felt on that awful morning. My hero, my unmet mentor, was dead.

I ran to tell my mother and asked to stay home from school. One of the many great qualities about my mom is that when you said you needed a day off from school, she would grant it. She knew we were under a lot of stress having to relocate so often. And that day, she knew I was dying inside.

I watched CNN all day long. Chris Curle and Don Farmer anchored a show called "Take Two," which provided extended coverage of Jessica's tragic death. Later would come the stories of Jessica's imperfections. I refused to believe any of them. I idolized this woman, and nobody could convince me she was depressed or addicted to drugs. How could she be? She was on national television and made lots of money—and after all, those were the two key ingredients to happiness.

I still own that original copy of Jessica's autobiography. It's a constant reminder of where it all began for me. Whatever her legacy with the public, Jessica Savitch left a teenage boy in Panama with a dream and the hope that he could achieve it.

Bad eyes and sunken chest be damned, I was heading for a broadcasting career and nobody would stop me.

Nobody did.

CHAPTER 1

The Perception Myth

Have you bounced around from pillar to post? Believe me, I can relate. During my adult years, I hopped from one radio station to another, each one offering a higher rung up the career ladder. Gradually, I worked my way up to the top and reached my goal of making fifty thousand dollars a year by the time I was thirty. In fact, I was bringing in much more than that.

Yet after the honeymoon period at each job wore off, none of the successes felt gratifying to me. My perception of inadequacy increased unabated. A bad day on the job would stick with me. I beat myself up over mistakes, never believing I was really good enough to be doing what I was doing. Even when receiving awards for my professional abilities, I would feel just a brief moment of excitement and then plunge back into depression.

Friends were few and far between. I didn't spend much time socializing because I was too busy working. The friends I did choose were misfits—in my mind, anyway. Many of them were overweight. Others had physical drawbacks. But I belonged with them. I felt we could relate because we all suffered from body image problems. My concave chest wasn't an issue with these friends.

I chose the misfits for another reason—to feel superior. And as terrible as it sounds, I would remind those "friends" of their shortcomings in order to make myself feel better. Of course, ultimately that only made me feel even worse.

I have to admit that I didn't like myself much. I had always heard the phrase, "you have to love yourself before you can love somebody else." But the problem was that I didn't love myself and didn't know *how* to fall in love with myself. Heck, I would have settled for just *liking* myself.

The years slipped by, and I continued to advance in work. Finally I ended up at ABC News in New York. This was *the* network—the big prize. But something was missing.

There I was, making very good money and broadcasting to hundreds of radio stations every hour. But there was a void. It was lonely at the top. I had few friendships, and they were strained. My insecurities would not allow me to get close to anyone. I was afraid they would find me out. They would realize I wasn't perfect and had many deep flaws. I kept even my closest friends at arm's length.

One day after an argument with a friend, I sat in my Manhattan studio apartment and realized that in every relationship I'd ever had, there was always a period of time when I didn't speak to the other person. Sometimes this would last for days, sometimes for months. There were even a couple of occasions where I'd never spoken to the person again.

Because of my perceived inadequacies, I had always pursued perfection. I had led people to believe that my life was perfect and if they wanted to be a part of it, they had to rise to my standards. I never wanted to appear vulnerable and so, when an argument surfaced with a friend, I became intransigent. I wasn't willing to admit I was wrong or that I actually needed friends in my life.

I sat lost in thought, contemplating my personal history. Finally it hit me. "It can't always be their fault; it must be mine." And at that moment, I made up my mind to make some changes. I vowed to appreciate the value of friendships and stop trying to compete with those friends. No, better: I would cheer them on to success. I would be happy for them and offer support when they were feeling down.

This may sound simplistic, but the difference was remarkable. For one, I felt better. Second, life seemed easier this way. My mother was one of the first to notice. When I visited her in Texas, she said, "You've changed and I like it."

It was true. I was friendlier and less sarcastic. I even enjoyed spending time with my nieces, and I was not a person who cared much for children. But this change wasn't easy. In order to embrace people, you have to let them in, and I had built up walls so high and thick that they made the Berlin Wall seem like a turnstile at a carnival. The barrier would take years to come down.

When you are insecure, walls provide protection. If you don't let people in, you don't allow them to reject you. That's really what it was all about—fear of rejection. I didn't want people to find out about my chest or poor eyesight or think that I might not be as smart as them. They might turn around and walk the other way.

But I made another pivotal discovery. When you show people who you really are, when you are absolutely authentic, they embrace you! Ask anyone looking for a perfect date, and usually they'll say they're looking for someone who's honest. They don't want secrets or façades; they want authenticity.

> When you are insecure, walls provide protection. If you don't let people in, you don't allow them to reject you.

"Real" people are not all that common. It's because society teaches us to hide or fix our blemishes. The images we see in television shows, movies, and magazines are perfect. They don't tell you about the airbrushing done to those photos. And when famous people make mistakes, the news media amplifies it. So there is intense pressure to be perfect, and to a large extent the public expects it.

It's all part of the Perception Myth. In the back of our minds, we know looks aren't everything, but because society sets a certain standard, we feel compelled to follow.

I don't remember my grandfather ever having hair on the top of his head. Yet my mother tells dozens of stories about his buying special shampoos and brushes to try and slow down his receding hairline. Even he succumbed to society's pressures, and that was back in the 1950s.

Grandpa Alfred was a big influence throughout my life, and I was with him the day his own life came to an end. My grandmother and I were sitting vigil in the hospital room when I heard a slight gasp. I quickly summoned a nurse, but when she took his vitals Alfred Wagner was dead. It was the first time I had witnessed a death and it was another step in my transformation. It made me ponder the meaning of life for the first time.

I thought about the finality of death. My grandfather would never again experience the joys of life. No longer would we share special moments together. I wondered whether he'd had any regrets.

If he'd had a chance to come back for one day, what would he have done? What would he have said to those closest to him? And what about the things that gave him stress in his life? Would they still have bothered him if he'd been given a second chance?

When Alfred died, I happened to be in the middle of the book *Don't Sweat the Small Stuff . . . And It's All Small Stuff.* Some people brush aside these types of books, dismissing them as pop psychology. But I find that sometimes the simplest messages are the most effective. With each example the book gave of someone under stress, I thought of Grandpa. And I realized that none of the stress of bills or squabbles with friends, relatives, and neighbors mattered now.

From that point on my mantra has become, "Will this issue matter on my deathbed?" Inevitably the answer is always a resounding no. Talk about taking a load off one's mind! That little book helped me a lot, but it didn't provide the ultimate answer. I continued to live with feelings of self-doubt and lack of self-worth. Years of low self-esteem are hard to erase, and it takes a lot of practice to view yourself in a positive light.

There's another school of thought that some are embracing, but I'm not one of them. The quote I've seen time and time again goes something like this: "embrace your perfectly imperfect self." I've also seen, "I am beautiful because I know my flaws." At first it sounds great! Many of us have something we dislike about ourselves. But I don't like the idea of trying to learn to love these little "flaws." I come from a school of thought that each of us is perfect, whole, and complete.

The idea of imperfection, whether you are willing to embrace it or not, makes something about you "wrong." So embracing imperfections would amount to the power of positive thinking, which is something else I don't subscribe to. When we use the power of positive thinking, we're talking ourselves into believing our lives or situations are better than what we actually think they are. Daily affirmations, for instance, can give us instant pick-me-ups. I see them virtually every day on someone's Facebook page. The trouble is that these affirmations wear off easily when you are faced with a challenge.

What works for me is taking inventory of the facts in my life, deciding what is factual and what is a narrative I'm adding. For example, you may believe your nose is too big. Chances are that you were ridiculed as a child, perhaps even still today, about the facial feature. The fact here is that your nose is a certain size, which won't change unless doctors perform surgery. Your internal narrative might be, "my nose is humongous, it's hideous, I look ugly," etc. This narrative is perception. There are people who find a larger nose attractive. Others might notice for a second, but would not avoid dating you because of this. Under the power of positive thinking, you would embrace the notion that your nose isn't perfect, but adds to your personality. And this is wonderful if you actually believe it. The trouble is that the next time someone makes a snarky remark about your nose, you revert back to your old way of thinking. This is because you don't believe the affirmations to be true, not in your gut.

Under the perfect, whole, and complete philosophy, you embrace yourself just as you are. This is the way you were made, so it's perfect. This is what nature had in mind for you. There will be people who like it and those who don't, and you will form your own opinions. Should you decide you want to change your nose, there's nothing wrong with that either. But don't think your nose is "wrong." And by changing your appearance, you are not making it "right." You are deciding to transform yourself, just as a person might do with a tattoo, piercing, or new hair color.

Young people need to get this message now rather than later. Well into my forties, I found an old picture in a photo album. It was a picture of me at about nine or ten years old, sitting on Santa's lap at the mall. They say a picture is worth a thousand words, but this one said so much more. In my opinion, it was priceless. I had seen this picture over the years, but it never spoke to me the way it did that time. I was struck by just how cute a boy I was back then, visiting with Santa. In fact, I posted the picture on Facebook for "Throwback Thursday." There were a number of "likes" and many comments, including words like "adorable" and "cute."

At the time the photo was taken, I did not think of myself in this way. Even though I had ditched my thick glasses, I still suffered from poor self-image. I was a miserable child, believing I was a freak of nature because of my terrible eyesight and my below-average grades in school.

This image stuck with me for decades until one day I found that picture and looked at it very differently. It was as if I were looking at someone else, rather than myself in that photo. I thought about how much time was wasted. The kid in this photo was just like any other his age—a big smile, a head full of hair, and a desire to be loved. I was not unattractive, as I had believed all those years. When I should have been socializing with others, I kept to myself. I was a loner. I thought I was ugly and unworthy of love. This is a terrible way to go through life and it's completely unnecessary.

This was a classic example of a misperception. I thought it was fact. As sure as I was sitting on that jolly old elf's lap, I was ugly and undesirable. And I was wrong.

Are you seeing the *real* you? Take another look in that mirror. Rather than finding the flaws, pick out your attributes. Dimples? A bright smile? What is it about you that others will find attractive? Moving toward a positive picture of yourself requires one to retrain the brain. Thoughts, as well as the way they travel, have to be altered.

When negative thoughts start to surface, find something positive to focus on. In time, this will become a new habit and your brain will begin to gravitate toward positive thoughts rather than negative.

Beware of the social media effect on our perception. It can obscure the images we have of others as well as ourselves. Nearly everyone gets caught up in the trap of the Perception Myth at some time or another. It's easy to do. If you are able to identify the myths, you can then address them and move on. Our thoughts about how we look, act, and fit into the world not only shape our characters, but our personal worlds as well. When we convey, either outright in speech or less directly, that we are less than worthy, others pick up on it and treat us as such. Low self-esteem can push people to excel, wanting to be bigger and better and not stop until they achieve their goals. But too often, it can hold people back, paralyzing them in fear. We then get stuck dreaming about moving forward with our lives, but can't bear to take risks in seeking out those goals.

It seems the Internet is providing some relief, though it may be short-lived. Through Facebook or Twitter accounts, we can share only the information we want people to see. We can create the characters we wish to be. A picture from a restaurant shows we're social. A status update about a wonderful opportunity on the horizon or even a simple "life is great" leads our followers to believe everything is right in our world and we are successful, social beings. This too can be a trap. It's great to share in the social media world—allowing those we might not otherwise keep in touch with to check in and see how we're doing. But it also allows us to live a sort of false life on the Internet—one that does not match with the one we're living in reality. This is creating a false perception among those who follow us. There's really no danger here aside from the fact we can get lost in this world and neglect our real one, along with associations with real people.

When I began dealing with reality and decided my life needed an overhaul, I started exploring the self-help section of my local bookstore. I read Eckhart Tolle and Dr. Wayne Dyer for a philosophical perspective. Joyce Meyer, Max Lucado, and Joel Osteen provided spiritual guidance. In all of their works, there was a common theme: move away from your ego and don't be so hard on yourself.

Great advice, but easier written than done. It's one thing for someone to tell you to do something. It's quite another for them to show you *how* to do it.

When I decided to write a book about my life and the lessons I've learned, I wanted to share some of the wisdom I've acquired over the years. But more importantly, I wanted this to be a how-to book as much as a self-help manual.

Every man, woman, and child has to learn that they are significant and that they matter. No human being is any more special than another. After all, we're all essentially the same—a combination of millions of cells. And science shows us that most of those cells are pretty much the same from human to human, with the occasional abnormalities we know as birth defects. When you feel significant, you are empowered. You believe anything is possible in your life.

I've learned a few lessons about accountability and responsibility that I will share. Understanding and embracing these two ideas is critical to making your life run smoothly and gaining the respect of others. Too often we hear excuses from our friends and relatives about why something went wrong or why they are unable to get ahead.

And, believe me, these are excuses. Holding oneself accountable can be a scary notion. You are acknowledging that a failure, or something you perceive to be a failure, is your fault. It's much easier to blame other people, outside sources, or your unfortunate circumstances.

By taking responsibility for your life, you are standing up and saying, "The buck stops with me." This can be a great motivator. Taking responsibility also means you get the satisfaction of success when you put yourself out there, take chances, and succeed. Taking chances is tied directly to self-esteem. When we don't think we're good enough, we tend to stay within our comfort zones. Stepping out of that zone is hard because we run the risk of rejection. But not taking a leap results in a stagnant, boring, and unfulfilled life, and who wants that?

Taking chances will also result in change, which can be scary. I'll share with you how change can be a good thing, even if the situation seems bleak at the time. You'll learn how to change your perception about change. The world is forever changing, and there's nothing we can do to stop it. Nothing in life is permanent, so get used to it. You'll hear me say that a lot. And to truly live a life of fulfillment, we must let go of our baggage and forgive those who have wronged us in some way.

What makes me an expert on all of this? You've heard the expression, "I've been around the block a time or two"? Well, let's just say this was my regular route. There was a time in my life when I thought I'd never find happiness and never be able to accept myself, but I found a new path—one that works. And I want to share that with you.

If any of this sounds like you, there's good news ahead. You have the ability to write or rewrite your narrative, and this book will show you, step by step, how to turn your life around.

Here, then, is my story and the lessons I learned along the way. The powerful lessons that finally made me realize I'd been living the Perception Myth.

CHAPTER 2

The Perception of You

Before you can transform your life, you have to know whom you're dealing with. While it may sound silly, the question must be asked, "Who are you?" Better yet, "Who do you *think* you are?"

You're most likely to answer with your occupation. "I'm a fire-fighter," you might say. Or a woman with small children could reply, "I'm a mother." A politician might throw his or her party affiliation out there—"I'm a Democrat." Our perception of ourselves is also wrapped around the sum of our experiences. For instance, if you were a bashful kid, you think of yourself as a shy person. If your grades were below average, you perceive yourself as not being very smart. Self-perception can be very inhibiting.

Mark Burnett, producer of the hit TV show *Survivor,* tells the story of how he ventured into selling T-shirts in Los Angeles. In his book, *Dare to Succeed,* Burnett explains, "I still saw myself as the immigrant boy trying to make good. That self-perception was limiting me, blinding me to other talents I might possess."

Burnett came to America with just six hundred dollars to his name. He took a job as a nanny and then moved into the T-shirt business. Burnett didn't feel comfortable making the switch because he did not perceive himself as a salesman. He quickly learned he was great at sales and, by widening his perception of himself, ended up selling program ideas to television executives.

Imagine the possibilities if you could open up the vision of who you are and what you are capable of doing!

Let me tell you about the time I discovered I had some artistic talent. My Los Angeles condo is beautifully decorated, and I'm proud to show it off. My friend is an interior designer who brought his expertise to this project. But just when we thought everything was in perfect order, we noticed the foyer had a rather dull piece of artwork. It was a piece that had been created by a family friend, so it held special significance. But opening my front door every night, I noticed it—something was missing.

My designer friend suggested that instead of buying a piece of artwork that would be appropriate for my foyer, we should create it ourselves. It needed to be a particular size and contain specific colors, which could have proven somewhat difficult to find.

I've never considered myself artistic—quite the reverse. As a child I was useless at art. Heck, it didn't help that I was color-blind. I'm a lot of things, but an artist is not one of them. Still, I decided to give it a shot. It was to be an abstract painting, and my friend assured me there was no wrong way to paint abstract art.

We began by painting a solid color as background and then added splashes of other colors all over the canvas. And would you believe—it turned out to be a magnificent piece of art! I posted a picture on

Facebook and racked up a heap of compliments from my friends. After basking in the glory of those accolades, I decided to try some painting on my own. It didn't exactly work. I wanted to capture my nephew's golden retriever as I remembered it, but its head ended up looking more like a duck's than a canine's. Obviously, painting images freehand was not my strong suit. I lacked the talent and imagination.

Not to be discouraged, I tried a different approach. I found a photo of my nephew's dog on his Facebook page and printed it out. Then I started painting, copying the photo. It was remarkable; for me anyway. By the time I finished, it actually looked like a dog and could pass for real artwork.

The point is—my original perception of not being an artist had been a myth. It was wrong. I had just needed to find a way to discover the artist inside of me. I was determined to create something on my own that could be appreciated. And now there is a place for me in the art world because I didn't stop at the first roadblock.

Don't be limited by what you think you can't do. It may just be your self-perception that's wrong. Take a chance and experiment; you might surprise yourself.

I believe we are all capable of doing many things, almost anything we desire, if we just try to access that side of ourselves. Notice how I became an artist in a matter of three painting sessions? It only takes an instant to create a new you!

Some people are more talented at painting than me, others are better singers, and I won't even talk about my lack of ability to play a musical instrument. But I decided to become an artist and the instant I made the decision, I *was* an artist.

Consider using this philosophy in your own life!

> Don't be limited by what you think you can't do. It may just be your self-perception that's wrong.

Less Than Worthy

As mentioned earlier, my father was a military man; he was with the armed forces for thirty years before retiring. He receives 75 percent of his pay plus cost-of-living increases. It's more than enough to retire on, but Dad has continued to work since leaving the military, which provides a very comfortable income for him and my mother. Dad is very active and can't sit around doing nothing. He'd be bored out of his mind.

But when they moved into an upper-middle-class neighborhood, my dad felt very out of place and uncomfortable. Until then, we'd mostly lived in military base housing, modest cracker box–type homes. Now my parents were in a neighborhood where the houses were large and lawns were as green as golf courses.

Dad felt out of his league. He believed his neighbors were somehow better educated and more sophisticated than he was. It took a lot of work on Mom's part to reassure him that they belonged in that neighborhood as much as anybody else living there. Over time, Dad got used to the community and now doesn't think twice about whether he belongs there.

You see, my father's perception of himself was that he was less than adequate. But it was a Perception Myth! No one else thought that; certainly not his neighbors. In fact, they may themselves have felt intimidated by my parents. After all, Mom and Dad had a nice house with a brand-new sedan and sports car in the driveway. They were living the American dream. Once my father was able to overcome his misperceptions, then he became happy and settled.

What do you perceive to be your shortcomings? Your station in life? Let that all go and know you can be whomever you wish. Just make the decision and *start living it.*

My Droopy Eyes and Awful Chest

If you want the truth, ask a homeless person. He or she has nothing to gain by making you feel good.

One of the reasons I was so passionate to be on television was to prove to myself that not only was I worthy and wanted, I was attractive. In my opinion, a TV station was unlikely to hire someone ugly or with a bad body.

While working in Oklahoma City, I met some friends for drinks at a local bar in the Bricktown section of the city. This was the entertainment district, consisting at the time mostly of bars and restaurants. I had parked my car and caught up with a few friends when a homeless man approached one of them, asking for money. They did not oblige. The man then approached me, uttering the unflattering words, "Man, you are ugly. You got your mother's eyelids." I smiled and pretended it didn't bother me, but I was hurting on the inside. This man had told me what he really thought, and I believed him.

Let's back up nearly twenty years. While in history class at Balboa High School in Panama, a classmate casually mentioned to me that I looked tired. She said my eyes were drooping. And for the next twenty years I obsessed about my droopy eyes. I looked in the mirror constantly and would try to open my eyes as wide as possible, but the homeless man, whom I would meet decades later, was right: my eyes were half-shut and I looked sleepy.

At the time, it was one girl's opinion and she probably never gave it a second thought. Be careful when commenting to someone. It may be inane to you, but could be devastating and long-lasting to the other person.

About five years before the homeless man entered my life, I visited KWTX-TV in Waco, Texas. I was an anchor at a radio station in Dallas and wanted to move into television. I needed the fix. I needed the validation that I thought TV would deliver. When I met with the news director—his name escapes me—he looked at a crude audition tape I had made and gave me some feedback. He said my delivery was strong, but there was something with the eyes . . . he couldn't put his finger on it. He did not have an opening at the time but said he would consider me for a job when something opened up.

I knew what he was talking about: those damned droopy eyes! Ugh, why couldn't I be average just like everybody else? I would ask myself.

A few years later, I called my friend Kent Harrell, who was a news director at a television station in Amarillo, Texas. I asked him if I could fly out and put an audition tape together. Kent's answer was, "Sure, but you will have to work for me all weekend, putting real stories together for our broadcasts." What? I was going to be on-air? On TV? I couldn't believe it.

I flew to Amarillo only to have the airline lose my luggage, which included shirts, ties, and sports coats. On Saturday, Kent allowed me to steal some of his clothes, and I went out with a photographer and shot two stories. One was a high school marching band contest, the other a fundraiser for a woman who needed a liver transplant.

That night, Kent and I sat in his apartment and watched my television debut. There I was on TV—a dream come true. I jumped up and down, oblivious to Kent sitting there watching me. I could not believe I was actually appearing on TV.

I did the same thing the following day and had my audition tape ready to go. When I was shopping it around, one news director told me I had a lazy eye and that it would probably prohibit me from anchoring in a big market or moving to a network, but I could have a job at his station.

Again the damn eyes! I couldn't get away from them. I wore glasses to help disguise the droopiness, but I wasn't sure it worked. Part of me believes I was determined to make it in television for the validation; another part thinks it was a form of self-torture. Knowing in my mind that I was less than ideal-looking, I went on forging ahead, and kept hearing comments about my eyes.

Years later, I would be doing on-camera stand ups for ABC News. National television had no problem with my eyes. The issue never came up.

Sometimes we look for evidence to support our poor self-perception. I did, and I found it. Had I looked for positive feedback, I would have found that instead: my friend Kent, a full-fledged news director, never mentioned an issue with my eyes.

On top of this, I had the concave chest to worry about. My mother started noticing something different about my chest when I was about ten or so. She's a natural worrywart who loves her children dearly. So when my chest failed to develop properly, my mother sought opinions. My first memory of this was a visit from my Uncle Kenny and Aunt June. My mom had me come over to the dining room table and lift my shirt. As she waved her hand over my chest, she asked, "Kenny, do you think this is normal?" Kenny's response was, "I don't think it's anything to worry about."

Mom didn't give up. She knew something was wrong and worried it might be a real health issue. She asked a doctor to take a look. He listened in his stethoscope as I breathed and determined I had pectus excavatum—Latin for "hollowed-out chest." He assured Mom that this would not impact my health, other than I might not have quite as much lung capacity as other kids my age did.

The message I received was that there was something wrong with me. My chest didn't look like other boys', and therefore I was deformed and different from my peers.

This, too, would haunt me for decades. It turns out that Mom was right to worry about the chest. More than thirty years later, I was diagnosed with Marfan syndrome. A friend in New York read a newspaper article that described the physicality of Marfan sufferers and, sure enough, I fit the bill: extremely long limbs, a gaunt face, possibility of pectus excavatum, etc. When she notified me of the possibility, I went to my doctor. For the most part, Marfan has no great impact on one's life sans one major problem: it can lead to aortic dissection in the heart, which can be fatal. Many people with this syndrome are never diagnosed, and their fatal heart failure comes essentially out of nowhere. I've been checked, and the heart looks good. So Mom was doing her job. I interpreted her concern as "something is wrong with me," but now I know it was simply my perception, not necessarily the truth.

As history would dictate, Mom then began her campaign of trying to convince me that my chest wasn't so bad. When I would mow the grass as a teenager, she would ask, "Why don't you take your shirt off and get some sun?" My response was typical for a teen: "because I don't want to."

Most of my life was spent in avoidance. I stayed away from swimming pools for the most part, except for the summer I earned my "advanced beginner" swimmer's badge from the American Red Cross. I spent nearly every day that summer in the pool at Whiteman Air Force Base in Knob Noster, Missouri. But every day I would wear my bathing suit along with a T-shirt, keeping fully dressed until I got to the edge of the pool. At this point I would take off the shirt and immediately jump in the water. I felt as though nobody could really make out my deformity while I was underwater.

Sitting at my desk in school, I would constantly tug at the middle of my shirt to sort of fluff it up and pull it away from my sunken chest. I truly felt ashamed and inadequate. I knew the pectus wasn't my fault, but somehow it didn't register. I felt inferior to other boys in school and therefore I kept to myself.

In my early twenties I discovered walking as not only the one exercise I liked, but one that cleared the mind or allowed me to daydream about my future.

It started with one walk around Town Lake (now Lady Bird Lake) in Austin, Texas. I worked at the local radio station, which was nearby. One day after work, I decided to head to the trails that ran alongside the water and was instantly hooked.

Not only am I a creature of habit, eating at the same restaurants and ordering the same items off the menus, I am a bit obsessive. So, weather permitting, I walked around Town Lake every single day that I lived in Austin. My headphones cranked out the sad country songs that I loved so much and my mind would wander. I dreamed of the day I would make it big—working at the network. My fantasies included the lavish apartment I would own and the fancy cars I would drive. It was a partial escape from reality. I say partial because my nagging chest never left me.

Before I began these walks, I would figure out which way the wind was blowing and then walk with my back to the wind. This prevented my T-shirt from being blown up against the sunken part of my upper torso and causing me embarrassment. So for the first half of each walk, I escaped reality. A nice breather. But when I made the loop and headed in the opposite direction, I faced the wind and constantly pulled my shirt out of the concave area of my chest.

My eyes would dart down when I would pass other walkers. I couldn't look them in the eyes because I was keeping a very dark secret. There was a part of me, as silly as it may sound, that felt if I didn't look at them, then they wouldn't look at me and notice the mangled upper body I had to live with.

I became obsessed with looking in mirrors to see if my chest was noticeable. Perhaps I thought by some miracle it would change. It never did. Having a physical disfigurement made me an expert at disguise, or so I thought. I would layer up in winter—the more layers in that concave area, the more the hole would be filled in.

Overall, I was not often made fun of by other kids—mainly because I never exposed my chest to them. It would happen occasionally in gym class or at the pool, but outside of that, my shirt never came off in front of others. But the few comments that were made were indelible marks.

As an adult, intimacy was difficult, so I avoided it. Rather than face possible rejection, I concentrated on my career. There were times I wished I had some other handicap, like an amputated leg or paralysis of both legs. My rationale was that these impairments would be immediately noticeable to anyone and everyone who came in contact with me. There would be no hiding it. And those who stuck around would be my true friends, accepting me in entirety.

I know today that I'm a very lucky person in that my chest does not impair me in any physical way. But back then was a different story, and I was a total mess. The problem with having something like a sunken chest is that you *can* hide it. That's a problem because when you hide things, you run the risk of someone finding out.

There's also the "reveal." When you do decide to join a friend at the beach, the shirt comes off and you don't know whether to explain it or not say anything and let them approach you about it. I lived my life in fear that people would reject me because of the way I looked. It was agonizing.

To give you an idea of just how much I despised and resented my body, I would not walk around my own apartment without a shirt, even though I lived alone. I slept with a shirt on and, aside from taking showers, my chest was covered up at all times. I couldn't bear to look at it.

In 1995, I was working in Dallas and decided to see a plastic surgeon. There were no Internet search sites like we have today, so very little information was available for those of us who suffer from pectus. Doctor Azouz told me he could make a custom silicone implant and stick it in my body and my chest would look perfectly normal. That's all I needed to hear.

I had had multiple operations on my eyes before the age of ten and vowed never to go through surgery again. But this was different. This was a life-changer. I would soon be "normal."

A few days later, the doctor unwrapped my bandages and revealed the chest. My parents couldn't believe it. My dad said it looked perfect, and Mom agreed. Several days later, the skin on top of my chest started dying. Apparently, there had not been much blood flow in the very center of my concave chest, so when the doctor pulled the skin away and stuck the implant in, the skin lost the very little blood it was getting. Doctor Azouz had me come in for a follow-up surgery. They would stretch the skin and sew up the part that had withered away.

I tried going back to work the week after and had a tough time of it. I was in deep pain. The implant was so heavy it rested on the top of my stomach, rubbing it every time I made a movement. This must have created some bruising on the top of my stomach because it hurt like hell. The wound started to reopen. There was a gaping hole in the middle of my chest and fluid was flowing out of it like a waterfall. I was scared, my mother was frightened, and I eventually told the doctor to remove the implant. I was devastated. Not only did this not work, but now I had a huge scar on top of my concave chest. It looked worse than it did before I started.

This was a time in my life so traumatic for both me and my family that my mother to this day doesn't like to talk about it. At this point I had pretty much given up. My life would be what it had always been: disguising my inadequacy and living a lie in hopes of never being found out. I had not let anyone close to me for fear of rejection. I even kept my family at a distance. It was safer this way because I wouldn't get hurt, I thought.

But my self-perception was based on other people's opinions. My chest was concave and a novelty to others because they didn't see it every day. Was it such an awful sight? Probably not.

The homeless guy and the girl in school saw my eyes as droopy. Others over the years have called them bedroom eyes and even sexy. It would be years before I realized that I had made myself out to be some sort of freak and that while I was unique, I wasn't necessarily inadequate.

Take a good look at yourself in the mirror. Appreciate that person and know that *you* decide your self-image. You are much more than a body or an occupation. You are a human being, capable of loving and being loved. Your only limitation is yourself.

The Opinion That Counts

Be careful not to allow the perception of others to influence who you are or your plans to succeed. Obviously, if your boss perceives you are doing something wrong or performing under par, he or she will say something and you'd better come to an understanding with that supervisor. However, when others offer their opinions of us, we need to keep in mind that these are simply perceptions and they may be false.

When I left ABC News after more than a decade with the company, someone in the industry wrote these words: "He was a tremendous news anchor. Didn't quite have the best pipes." Those of us in the industry refer to voices as pipes. I agree with the man's critique. I knew early on I didn't have that deep voice that is so common among many old-time broadcasters. I had to make my voice work, and so I concentrated on inflection and sentence structure to keep the listener's attention. This media "expert" added this to his critique: "[Wheelis] was totally unflappable. He never hesitated, paused, or flubbed a line. Ever." Wow! This man thinks my delivery was perfect. That's far from the case. We're all human so we will make mistakes, and I certainly made my share on live radio. But this one person's perception was that I never stumbled on the air. Since I have recordings of my mistakes as well as those newscasts that I consider exceptional, the man's perception is simply a myth.

The point is that you may or may not agree with the way people think about you and that's okay. In fact, I encourage you to note what they're saying but stay true to yourself. You will never please all of the people all of the time, nor should you attempt to do so. It's futile.

As a network anchor, I found myself being treated as a star on some levels. When I'd speak with news people at radio stations around the country, they would let it be known they were impressed with my credentials and expressed gratitude for having the opportunity to speak with me. They treated me as though I were special. The fact is that many of those folks are just as capable as me, or perhaps even more talented. It's easy to allow this to go to your head and inflate your ego.

But just as they were complimenting me, a listener might be complaining about the way I reported a story. It seems to balance itself out. For many years I would ride high after someone lauded me with compliments only to find myself depressed when there were complaints. Along with the depression came anxiety. Was I not good enough? Was I even capable of doing the job? Those are just a couple of the self-doubting questions that would arise. It took many years to finally realize I was talented and valuable and that opinions would differ.

Here's another example. Have you ever gone to see a movie that critics panned but you loved? It happens all the time. Some of the sillier comedies and far-fetched sci-fi flicks get scathing reviews from those who are supposed to be experts, but fans of the genres enjoy these films. Take a look at a website like *www.rottentomatoes.com* and you'll often notice a gap between the critics' rating and the audience rating.

I happen to like romantic comedies, and more often than not these movies are formulaic in their storytelling. It's as if I can predict what's about to happen. The critics don't like this approach, but I'm still a sucker for a happily-ever-after ending. I usually find myself wiping away a tear or two as well. So what if the movie doesn't meet the elite filmmaking standards?

Car chases are also a favorite of mine, so the *Fast & Furious* franchise was a must-see for me. The dialogue can be trite and even phony, but I love the action in these movies. Critics can pan them, but they make big bucks at the box office. If you like the genre, that's all that matters.

And since I'm a car nut, I'll compare this to the auto industry. There are people who love Ford products while others prefer Chevy. It doesn't mean either brand is awful. The only opinion regarding you that really matters is your own.

Lesson:

1. Take note of those who influenced your self-perception.
2. Know that you can succeed despite your perceived flaws.
3. Stop collecting evidence to support your poor self-image.
4. Decide you are more than a body, occupation, or a culmination of your history.

CHAPTER 3

Changing Your Self-Perception

Maybe you *should* jump the fence to see for yourself whether the grass truly is greener on the other side. We tend to look at other people's lives and believe they somehow are happier and wealthier and have an easier time of it. But this is our perception. After a more thorough examination, you may find they have struggles greater than yours.

One of the most common examples is the single woman versus the married woman. I've heard time and again from my single female friends about how they wish they could find that special someone and settle down. The single woman believes her life would then be complete. Consequently she's envious of the married woman.

The married woman enjoys her life but wonders what it would be like to be single again. She sees the single woman eating out with friends, having fun, and dancing on the weekends while she sits wistfully at home on Friday nights because her husband is exhausted. Each woman believes the grass is greener on the other side.

Now, let me go a step further and pose this question to you: how do you even know that grass is green? Or that the sky is blue?

The answer, of course, is that society has denoted a certain color green and another blue. Pretty cut and dry. But what if you are color-blind like me? You have a distorted concept of blue or green or brown or red. Even though most people tell you the colors are spectacular and green is green and blue is blue, you simply have to take their word for it because you can't see the difference.

Most of us look at the world through our own lens, believing what we see and what we've learned to be the absolute truth. We can view it no other way. But maybe, just maybe, we haven't been open to other ideas. I'm not suggesting you change your politics or morals or anything of the kind. What I'm asking is that you at least consider that there may be something you haven't considered. Life comes in many shades.

I've had eye problems since I was a baby, but my vision has remained constant over the years until recently. The last time I visited the optometrist, he told me my long-distance vision had improved and wrote a new prescription for contact lenses. Once the contacts arrived, I popped them in and could read signs off in the distance just fine. However, it was a weaker prescription than my last one, so it was more difficult to read books or texts. Everything was a little bit smaller.

> The first step toward piercing the Perception Myth is to consider that your perception may not be accurate.

For the first time in my life, I found myself questioning how big a penny really was. A car key looked different, as did an inch on a ruler. Everything looked smaller, and suddenly my whole world was different. I had thought for sure that I knew exactly what an inch looked like, but now that wasn't the case.

So I began to wonder what everyone else was seeing. Could they have known the inch was smaller? Or did objects appear larger to them? There are so many different eyeglass prescriptions out there; we may all be looking at the world in different ways. Yet we believe that our way alone is the truth—the absolute truth.

The first step toward piercing the Perception Myth is to consider that your perception may not be accurate. It may not be the truth. And it's not just about appearances; we have different views about life and the way we think it should work.

At six feet three inches, I am a tall man. As silly as it may sound (and no pun intended), I sometimes lose sight of the fact that I'm tall. When I'm at a social event, such as the theater or a party, I don't consciously think about my height. I think I blend in. But others in the room see me as usually towering over everybody else. They perceive a tall man. Only when I'm standing next to a short person and have to slightly bend over to hear what they're saying do I become aware of my tallness.

I was reminded of this recently at a colleague's wedding. I was walking around and chatting with different folks, not giving much thought to my height, but later when I looked at the wedding photos, I was shocked. Compared to the rest of the crowd I was much taller than anyone else in attendance.

This is one example of how one's perception is sometimes flawed.

My friend Rob has told me he was never a very smart guy. He struggled in school. But as an adult, Rob wrote, produced, and starred in an independent film, which was brilliantly made. In spite of his achievement, Rob still thinks he is lacking intelligence and that he has to work harder. Yet my first impression of him in person and after watching his movie was that he must be pretty smart to be able to come up with a plot and dialogue and assemble the people necessary to make the film.

He is currently working on a feature movie that he wrote, directed, and starred in. I've seen a rough-cut scene and it looks amazing. I don't have the skill to put something like this together, yet it comes easily for Rob because he has the passion for it, he's intelligent, and he has learned the skill of moviemaking.

But no matter what I say to Rob, he's the only one who can change his thinking and his self-perception. Rob has a choice to make. He can believe he is an intelligent human being or continue thinking he's not smart enough and hold himself back.

This isn't about positive thinking or affirmations. You have to realize that you are fine just the way you are. You don't need fixing or changing. You have to believe this in your core. You have to see it for yourself. Loving yourself is nothing more than accepting who you are.

We are a country of citizens who love to eat. And we spend hundreds of millions of dollars on diet plans and gym memberships each year to try and fit the images we see in the media: perfect chiseled bodies with barely any fat.

We've come to realize these bodies are not the norm. And with social media, pictures of movie stars without airbrushing have been shared across the Internet, allowing us to see that the famous are very much like you and me.

Of course there are medical standards for height and weight proportion. And if you are staring at a large person in the mirror, isn't this the correct perception? The good news is you get to create your own perception of yourself, and if you have bigger hips and thighs than the average person, you decide whether it's a problem.

Perhaps a checkup with the doctor is in order to make sure there aren't any health issues, but aside from that, you decide whether you feel good about that image in the mirror.

If you decide to shed a few pounds, that's okay too. It doesn't mean you are self-loathing and ugly; it means you desire to make some physical changes. You decide what that number on the scale is going to be and what you are comfortable with. The same goes for cosmetic procedures. These droopy eyes of mine are something I'm comfortable with now. But had I chosen to have my eyelids lifted, that would have been perfectly fine.

This isn't about whether or not droopy eyes are attractive in our society; it's about whether I have a problem with the way I look. The key is to accept and love yourself as you are; then if you desire to make some changes, have at it. There's nothing wrong with making adjustments, just don't beat yourself up over a perceived flaw.

That One Thing

If you are looking for what's wrong, rest assured, you'll find it. We all seem to have that one "thing" that bothers us. And for some, it's not just one thing, but many. Poor self-esteem holds too many people back. Don't allow this to cast a shadow over your dreams and goals.

My friend Stephen Katz is an actor who has appeared in those clever Super Bowl ads that tens of millions of Americans watch. In my opinion, Stephen has made the big time.

Before his success in commercial work, Stephen lived in Arizona. Lots of friends told him it would be difficult, if not impossible, to make it in Hollywood. But Stephen was determined, and his hard work and some acting classes paid off. He was able to bring in enough money to support himself as a working actor. He didn't consider failure an option. A common question Stephen gets is, "What is your secret?"

As Stephen puts it, "We have the power to achieve anything we want and to obtain our hearts' deepest desires. What stops us isn't a lack of opportunity or education, but rather a lack of deep belief in ourselves that we are capable and deserving enough to truly have our life be the way we dream it to be."

That's powerful stuff. Where others have given up, Stephen has put himself out there, and it's paid off.

You are worthy and capable, and when you start to believe that, your life can be limitless.

YOU *ARE* SIGNIFICANT!

Most of us are striving to make a mark in the world. We want to be significant, yet too many of us believe we are insignificant. Are you the person your boss thinks you are? Did your fifth grade teacher have you pegged right? What do total strangers make of this person you stare at in the mirror each morning?

My point is that we all come up with a way to define ourselves— shy, extroverted, smart, dumb, funny, boring, cute, ugly . . . you get the picture. But our definition may be distorted by events in our past.

Take my friend John, for instance. Here's basically what he wrote on Facebook: "I've been a disc jockey and talked on the radio to thousands of people. I've been a news anchor and, again, talked to thousands of people. I've been onstage and presented major artists and concerts. But today in front of three people at a job interview, I suddenly became nervous 'little' John from a small town in Oklahoma, with sweaty palms and a nervous laugh."

Do you get it? John is feeling the same way I felt when I arrived in New York for a job interview. Many people think this way. It's as if that image we had of ourselves as kids rears its ugly head and we're doomed.

Changing Your Self-Perception

In 1997, my friend Billy came to visit me in New York and stayed for over a month. I rather enjoyed the company because I hadn't made many friends there. Billy was a big talker. He and I had met back in my early days of radio and I looked up to him. He spoke a good game and always had a better way of running a radio station than the current management. His ego was pretty healthy too. "I could run circles around that guy," he would say.

So when Billy found himself out of work, I suggested he go on a road trip with me. We would drive my Mercedes (a trophy of my success at the time) to New York City. I had parked it in Texas with my folks when I got the job in the Big Apple.

Billy agreed, and off we went. We had a wonderful time, stopping at Bob's Big Boy restaurants all along the route. Billy was a huge fan of the place and couldn't drive past one of those diners without paying a quick visit. Sometimes we would finish a meal and get back on the highway only to see a sign for another Bob's Big Boy at the next exit. Inevitably we would stop and amuse ourselves at the thought of being so silly. I still have the pictures we took outside one of the restaurants, standing next to a life-sized Big Boy.

After we got to New York, I told Billy of two job openings I knew about and lined up interviews through my radio contacts. But Billy never showed up for either. I came back to my apartment one night to find him drunk. And when we began to discuss his no-show, I found out who Billy really was. He broke down crying, admitting he was too scared to show up. He didn't think he was good enough to work in the big city.

It was a shock to my system. There it was—the Perception Myth! It had fooled me well. I had thought this guy was confident—overconfident, even. But it was all a façade. He was the scared little child who lives inside all of us.

The frightened child survives in us because we were constantly fed damaging messages growing up. Adults told us how inadequate we were, children teased us, and we even told ourselves we weren't good enough.

I challenge you to start thinking of yourself as significant.

I have heard motivational speaker Tony Robbins say that it's human nature to want to be significant. He points out that one reason kids join gangs is to feel special or important. His example is alarming: "Imagine I'm from the wrong side of the tracks. On a scale of one to ten, I'm a one in terms of my significance to you. If I put a gun to your head, I suddenly become a ten in significance." Robbins believes this is one reason crime will continue.

Low self-esteem, the feeling of insignificance, is one of the greatest problems facing this country. Imagine if we could all feel good about ourselves and be confident in pursuing our dreams. There would be many more successful people running around this planet.

By simply being alive, you *are* significant! And all that baggage you're carrying is nothing more than an illusion. You are only shy if you choose to be. You are only awkward if you say you are. Try dropping the labels and just be yourself in front of people. You may be amazed at how they respond to you. And if one person rejects you, so what?

You don't like everyone you meet—so why should everyone you meet like you?

As I explained earlier, I was born with a condition that sometimes doesn't reveal itself until the age of ten or so—pectus excavatum. Essentially the cartilage in the middle of your chest never forms and doesn't harden properly. For all intents and purposes, I have a sunken chest. I was ultra-sensitive about it, as are most people who suffer from pectus. It made me feel insignificant and less of a man.

Though the condition is fairly common, you don't see many sufferers out in public. That's because most of us shy away from communal swimming pools or other places where men generally take their shirts off.

In junior high school, I dreaded the "shirts/skins" basketball games. The coach would arbitrarily point a finger at each kid and say either "Shirts," which meant you could leave your shirt on for the game, or the dreaded "Skins," which meant you had to remove your shirt. That was how P.E. teachers kept track of the two teams on the court.

I trembled with the anticipation and made myself sick over it. Sometimes I went to the nurse's office pleading sickness just to get out of class. That day the kid in my class saw my chest and said, "it looks like a bowling ball hit your chest. I cringed. There were some chuckles, I recall, including a bit of laughter from my own mouth. But inside I was crying.

One summer I spent the day swimming at my sister's house. Even around my family, I was so protective and secretive about my chest, which my six-year-old nephew didn't know about. Leave it to youngsters to be completely honest. He saw my concave chest and said, "B, there's a hole where your heart should be."

It was a profound statement from such a small creature. Sure, there was an indentation in my chest, but along with that came a whole lot more. I had never allowed myself to love others because I felt unworthy. I also had a tremendous fear of rejection. After all, nobody wants a freak.

A couple of years ago I enrolled in a transformational workshop called The Landmark Forum. There, I was finally able to come to terms with my chest, learning that everybody has something about themselves that they don't like. Fellow participants reminded me that I had other qualities that many would appreciate. The chest was just one part of a bigger package.

There was obviously more involved in this perspective change about my chest, but the bottom line was that I had obsessed over one part of my body and used it to judge myself without giving anyone a chance to get to know me intimately. In other words, I had defined myself by the irregularity of my chest. I had allowed my perception of self to identify me.

The truth of the matter is that people *will* judge you partly by your looks. There are laws of attraction. I may not like a big nose, or you may not like a small one. By the same token, there's a good chance someone won't like my chest, but that doesn't mean it will turn everybody off.

Another important thing I learned was not to beat myself up over it and not to blame myself for it. I was born with this condition and there's nothing I can do about it. It's not a good thing or a bad thing. It simply is what it is. There is something truly empowering about knowing and accepting that.

Abandon "Hope," Create Luck

Maintaining hope can provide courage for a person to persevere through hard times. Martin Luther King Jr. once said, "If you lose hope, somehow you lose the vitality that keeps life moving, you lose that courage to be, that quality that helps you go on in spite of it all." But Doctor King also knew that hope alone is not a life strategy. It would not get the job done. The civil rights movement needed more than hope. It needed action.

As I was walking through the MLK museum in Memphis, it was clear just how much work it took for black Americans to obtain equal rights under the law. Rosa Parks refused to give up her seat on the bus to a white person. One act by one woman had such an impact on the movement. Four African-American college students refused to leave a Woolworth's lunch counter without being served. The protests that followed led to desegregation at the eatery.

When President Obama was elected in 2008, he ran on a campaign of hope. But hope didn't get him to 1600 Pennsylvania Avenue. Action did. Hope is not a long-term strategy. Those who supported Obama may have felt a sense of hope, but it was their action—showing up at the polls—that got him elected. Had many of Obama's supporters just hoped he would be elected and sat at home on Election Day, John McCain would have won the election.

I don't say this as a partisan. I don't care about your politics. But as a former political correspondent, I simply point out the facts in that election.

Whether it's a grand movement, political campaign, or just ordinary folks' lives, hope alone won't accomplish our goals because hoping for something doesn't make it real. You have to act. Luck can be part of anyone's success, but you have to work hard to lay the groundwork.

As a student in elementary and even junior high school, I was always nervous on test day. My teachers gave plenty of notice about tests and told us time and again to study. I didn't. And as a result, on test day I hoped I would pass. Hope was not enough, as I found out on more than one occasion. Hope would not get me a passing grade, but action would. By studying, I would prepare myself for the questions faced on the quizzes. It sounds simplistic, and it is, but I didn't know it at the time. I was being lazy. I didn't want to study. I'd rather have spent time hanging out with friends. And I caused myself a lot of grief. By my junior year in high school, I finally figured it out. I knew if I wanted to graduate and go on to college I needed better grades. I started studying and found that tests were easy to pass. My grades dramatically improved and so did my self-esteem.

So what about your own life strategy? Will you hope for a promotion? Will you hope for more income? Will you hope to win the lottery? It all takes action, even the lotto. You must buy a ticket before you can win. The same holds true for other aspects of your life. If you want the promotion, you must lay the groundwork. You make your boss aware of your contributions and let him or her know how your assets benefit the company.

Do you feel lucky? Dirty Harry asked the question for a different reason. Trust me, I'm no Dirty Harry. I ask the question because my friend Pablo posed it to me after I had started writing this book. He wondered whether my successes in life were a direct result of hard work, the right attitude, just plain luck, or a combination of the three.

This I had to ponder for a while. Did I consider myself lucky? There was the time I got hired for a TV job in Waco, Texas, without an ounce of television experience. The news director was a former radio guy and took to me right away. That could be considered luck.

My love for gambling comes from my mother, who got the bug from her mother. I remember taking Grandma to the riverboat casino in St. Louis. "Gram, I'll be back to check on you in a few minutes," I said as I left her at a bank of slot machines.

It wasn't twenty minutes later that I showed up and asked how she was doing. Grandma was putting coins into a machine and simply said, "I just hit on that one and I'm waiting for them to pay me out." Gram had just hit a two-thousand-dollar jackpot. While the slots were fun, bingo was really her game. She loved the challenge of playing many cards at once and couldn't get enough of the camaraderie that goes with such social events. There too, Florence was lucky.

My mother started playing poker at family gatherings well before she was ten years old. And often she'd come home with some extra money. That meant a lot because she grew up poor, living in a farm house that lacked insulation. The kitchen was on the front porch and there was no indoor plumbing. That came after my mother entered high school.

Mom still loves to gamble. When she and my dad visited me in New York some years ago, I took them to Atlantic City to gamble. I gave my mother my player's club card to insert into the slot machine. This keeps track of how much money you spend, which is how you build up comps.

By the end of the weekend, my mother had spent so much money that I was elevated to the Bengal Club. This meant access to a private bar and buffet in the casino. Mom returned to Texas, after having paid for the entire trip, with an extra ten grand in her pocket. Diana Wheelis is lucky.

I haven't done so badly myself. I have a full carat diamond ring and joke that Donald Trump bought it for me. It was paid for by winnings from the Trump Taj Mahal in Atlantic City.

So could it be that I'm also lucky in my career?

After much thought, I've concluded that luck does exist and can be part of anyone's success, but if you look at a person's entire career, you'll find a pattern that leads me to believe we create much of our luck.

One of my biggest breaks in radio came when the Texas State Network in Dallas hired me. I was a news director in the city of Bryan at the time. This was a big promotion. A few years before this offer, I was in Austin. When I would show up at some news conferences I would run into Glynda Chu, a reporter and anchor from a competing radio station. Glynda will be the first to tell you equipment is not her specialty.

One day when I arrived, Glynda was fiddling with her recorder and couldn't get it to work. I helped her out. And subsequently, just about every time we saw each other in the field, I would set up her equipment for her. What was I thinking? She's the competition. You don't help the competition, right?

I believe in being competitive, but consider this: we were both at a news conference. This was a public event. I was not going to scoop her on a story. So why not do a good deed?

One day while I was working in Bryan, Texas, I got a phone call from Glynda. There was excitement in her voice. She said, "I was just promoted to news director and guess what the first thing I'm going to do is?" She went on to say she was hiring me as an anchor.

Did she want me to come up for an interview? Nope. Glynda said she knew my work and that I was good people and asked when I could start. That wasn't luck. That was me being a genuinely nice guy and getting the reward for it later. Glynda would help me get a TV job years later. She was one of the best bosses I've ever had. Not a day went by when Glynda wouldn't stop by my workstation and tell me that I was "stellar." That was her favorite way to describe my job performance and I loved her for it.

ABC News promoted me to the afternoon/evening anchor shift several years ago. Many people look at me as lucky. It's one of the best, if not *the* best, jobs in the radio news business. Was I lucky to get it? Perhaps, but I created that luck.

First I spent several years, more than four, working the overnight shift. People don't mention that when they talk about my luck. The graveyard shift at a network news organization is a great gig for your career, but let's face it: the hours suck. I spent years sleeping all day and working all night and then trying to adjust to a normal schedule on the weekend, only to revert back to the odd hours come Sunday night. This was an opportunity to prove to my bosses that I had the talent and drive to handle this position and anything else that came along.

My predecessor, one of the greatest talents in this business, surprised everybody when he decided to step down. Gil Gross took a job as a talk show host in San Francisco. When he left, it created an opportunity for me to move up. You see, there wasn't much luck involved, at least not from my perspective.

Success is based more on laying the proper groundwork. Figure out what you want to do and make a plan. Sometimes there are obstacles and you need to adjust the plan. That's okay, but stay focused, make the right contacts, pay your dues if necessary, and reap the rewards.

Want to be lucky? Then get to work.

Lesson:

1. Consider that your self-perception may be wrong.
2. Embrace yourself as you are. Self-acceptance is important.
3. Realize that action gets results. Take action to get what you want.

CHAPTER 4

Tap Into Your Inner Greatness

How we love the rich and famous. We put them up on pedestals so high that our arms can't reach. And then we tell ourselves that's unattainable for us. Many believe that celebrities, politicians, and the just plain rich are something special. They have something inside that we do not. They have what it takes to get to that level.

Part of this thinking is true. They do possess a certain something. But so do you!

This took me years to realize. When I was a cub reporter covering the state capitol in Austin, Texas, I was deeply intimidated at news conferences. I felt the other reporters—those I perceived to be more successful—were better than me. And when it came to ask a question of a politician, I became a tongue-tied introvert.

That changed one holiday season when all Capitol reporters were invited to the governor's mansion for a Christmas party. Ann Richards was governor back then—a feisty, white-haired, grandmotherly type. She was always pleasant but firm in news conferences.

I headed to the mansion, nervous as I could be. I had always been awkward when it came to socializing and this was no different. At least I would know a few people there. My date was Davee Benson, an old friend who really wanted to meet the governor.

As we made the rounds, the governor came up to me and said "Brad, I'm so glad you could make it tonight." She had called me by my name! As soon as that thought passed through my head, I realized we were wearing nametags.

But Governor Richards came up to me again later and asked if I had tried the chocolate cake. She highly recommended it. And she asked where Davee was. She had remembered Davee's name. I was impressed and realized for the first time that this very powerful woman was a typical person deep down. I left the mansion feeling on top of the world.

Some years later I met former first lady Rosalynn Carter. She visited KRLD radio where I worked to talk about Habitat for Humanity with one of our talk show hosts. After I delivered the news update during the show, we went to a commercial break and I greeted Mrs. Carter.

To my astonishment, the former first lady drawled in her inimitable southern dialect, "You have a lovely voice." I was shocked, which she must have seen on my face. I never really believed I was talented or had much of a voice. I had always thought my success was due to my determination.

The commercial on the air was about a product called Squirrel Away. It evoked a memory in Mrs. Carter, who launched into a story about having squirrels in her attic and how the former president himself had tried to get rid of them. She said he had become frustrated after several attempts and hired someone else to do the job. After I left the studio, it dawned on me that Mrs. Carter was a normal person, just like me.

And then there was former President George W. Bush. Back when he was governor of Texas, I was working in Dallas and had asked his office if we could get a quick interview with the governor while he was visiting The Ballpark in Arlington. They told me to stand by and wait and they would try to squeeze something in. Sure enough, someone from the governor's press office eventually told me I could see him, but it had to be quick.

I walked into the office of Tom Schieffer—the president of the Texas Rangers at the time. Tom wasn't there, but Governor Bush was. He greeted me with a smile and a firm handshake—very much a Texan. Then he asked if I minded waiting a minute while he changed out of jogging clothes into something more formal.

When he'd finished he came over and said, "Brad, what can I do for you?" I conducted a short interview and was on my way. A now-familiar thought ran through my mind. This guy was normal and not afraid to be on my level.

Despite the media's attempts to disparage him during the eight years he was president, I found Mr. Bush to be an intelligent man with a pleasant disposition and a wonderful sense of humor. Somehow that never translated on camera, but he was and is a nice guy, no matter your politics.

There were many more high-profile people I met along the way, and with each encounter I became more aware of the fact that these individuals had grown up just like the rest of us, but had somehow managed to tap into their inner greatness.

Greatness isn't reserved for the precious few; it's inside all human beings. It just needs to be accessed.

Oprah Winfrey is another example. She is arguably the most powerful woman in America, but she started from humble beginnings. She had the drive to get an education and become a news reporter. Eventually she would star in the film *The Color Purple*, which earned her an Oscar nomination. Backstage at the Academy Awards that year, Oprah felt like a fish out of water. Nobody knew who she was. Soon that all changed and she went on to host the most popular national talk show in history.

Oprah was successful because she had the drive and determination to succeed. But she also discovered her inner greatness—and became hugely successful by being herself. The audience found Oprah to be authentic. When she started doing away with sensational subjects and honed in on topics designed to help improve people's lives, her talk show's ratings took off. Being genuine is extremely powerful.

Greatness isn't reserved for the precious few; it's inside all human beings. It just needs to be accessed. The trouble is that we grow up being told that such fame and fortune are out of reach and that we are less than stellar. The reality is that politicians and celebrities all shared early traits similar to ours. They had to take out the trash and do other chores; they went to school, played kickball, and did the same things the other kids in the neighborhood did. These people were not manufactured by perfect parents, nor did they grow up in perfect homes.

Let's look at President Obama again. He grew up without a father, living with his grandparents in Hawaii. Obama has said he didn't make the best grades in school. In his speeches, he's told students that he wishes he had paid better attention in class, even though eventually his grades improved and he progressed to an Ivy League college.

The president became a community organizer in Chicago and went on to run for elected office. He *built* a political career for himself. His life could have gone in another direction, but Barack Obama made wise choices, befriended the right people, and carried himself in such a way that people were drawn to him. They felt a sense of confidence emanating from this man. That's what drew people to him and helped propel Obama into the national spotlight.

Having covered many presidential elections during my career, I can think of none that stood out more than the historical election of 2008. When the campaign first started, the pundits said former first lady Hillary Clinton was the shoo-in. Her husband, former President Bill Clinton, knew how to mount winning campaigns and would get her elected; she had the name recognition and the country was ready for a woman, they said.

The pundits told us Barack Obama could not win—not even the Democratic nomination. They claimed the country wasn't ready for a black man to lead. They said his name was difficult to pronounce and asserted he hadn't had enough time in federal office. It was a long, vigorous battle, and Clinton would not throw in the towel until very late in the game. The brutal campaign ended with the first black president being elected.

The point of this story is that it was not a certainty that Obama would be elected to the highest office in the land. He had to work for it. He had to endure accusations, ridicule, and even hatred. A very normal guy from an average background had accomplished what only forty-three men in history had done. He had become president of the United States.

We all possess greatness, we just have to figure out how to tap into it. That's what separates the highly successful from the average.

Don't Beat Yourself Up!!

The first step toward finding your inner greatness is to stop being so hard on yourself.

I beat myself up most of my life, well into my adult years. I never thought I was good enough, handsome enough, outgoing enough, or even talented enough. This was all a misperception. I look back at photos and realize I was a pretty good-looking kid. I listen to tapes of my early years in radio and realize I did possess a natural aptitude for talking on the air. But when you don't realize that, you present obstacles for yourself.

For at least the first half of my career, I did a lot of air-checking. That is, essentially I recorded every broadcast on a special tape recorder at the radio station. The recorder only came on when my microphone was switched on. This left out all the commercials and sound bites and reporter pieces we aired each day, leaving only the parts of me speaking into a microphone. Each evening I would listen to the entire day's broadcast and critique myself. It was never good enough. I found words I should have emphasized but didn't. I found my voice was too high-pitched or unnatural. And I vowed to work harder the next day.

It would be many years later when I would find my voice and realize that I was pretty good at what I did, so I didn't need to constantly evaluate my performance. Don't get me wrong, I still occasionally air-check to make sure my sound is consistent and to see if there's anything that needs attention. But I don't do it often, and I certainly don't obsess over it. I recommend people assess their performances because we need to do that in order to improve. But one must do it from a healthy perspective, knowing you are good enough and that it is for enhancement, not an overhaul.

In my early broadcast days, these air-check sessions were nothing more than a self-hating pity party. I would tell myself I wasn't good enough and didn't have the talent to be a successful broadcaster. I felt that way even as I was anchoring the news in big markets like Dallas and New York. Some of my friends in the business envied me and my position, and yet I felt like a loser. My perception was that I was still that kid with the big glasses who was too shy to talk to anyone. What business did I have to be on the radio? I would ask myself.

Nothing could have been further from the truth. I was qualified and talented enough and I deserved the position I was in. But it would take years to realize this.

Comparisons Are Odious

The next step to achieving greatness is to run your own race. Never mind the others. During those early years, I was always comparing myself to my colleagues and peers. I felt I wasn't as talented or well-rounded as those working beside me.

Don't allow this kind of thinking.

I began my career in broadcasting in high school. I was a bit of a phenom, praised for my early start in the business—my hustle had paid off. I started college while continuing to work full-time. One day it dawned on me the reason I was getting a degree was to get my foot in the door and start my career. I realized I already had my foot in the door and was working my way up. I decided to leave college before completing a degree. This haunted me for much of my career. Would people think I'm less intelligent because of my lack of degree? When people would ask about my major in college, I would tell them which "path" I took, though I never mentioned a degree.

Somewhere in the recesses of my mind I must have believed I was not as smart as my colleagues for not having pursued a diploma. At any rate, I allowed this to feed into my self-perception. I was terrified of being "found out." This is something the late ABC newsman Peter Jennings dealt with. Peter was open about the fact that his formal education was lacking; some colleagues say it forced him to push harder to get the story and get it right, as if he had something to prove. Peter was an amazingly intelligent man who knew more about the world than most and who made millions of dollars a year, yet he had a self-image problem. Wealth does not insulate us from the Perception Myth.

So self-esteem (our self-perception) can be our best friend or our worst enemy. Those with a healthy self-esteem believe in themselves and aren't afraid to take risks. Rejection may hurt, but it's tolerable and part of life. Those with poor self-esteem can't handle the rejection and add this to the list of "what's wrong" with them. And here's where it gets worse: our perception becomes our reality. We are what we believe. That's why it is imperative that you reframe your thinking and realize that you are capable of great things and that you are just as good as anyone else.

Our whole world is predicated on our own self-perception. And it's not just what we think about ourselves, but how we view the world. If our self-perception is skewed, we see things differently. We may not participate because we feel we don't belong. We may resent others because we feel they are better than we are. There can be an inner battle between feeling worthy and worthless. This is only perception, and it can change when you are ready.

Work at your own pace; worry about what *you* want and how *you* want to get there. You don't need to keep up with the Joneses, whether it be the car you drive, the clothes you possess, the house you live in, or the job you have at the moment.

I'm an avid car enthusiast; I got that from my father. We love all types of automobiles and the thrill that comes from driving them. And there's nothing wrong with owning a nice car or, indeed, several, as long as you are doing it for the love of cars and not primarily to impress other people.

I bought my first Mercedes-Benz strictly to impress people, I admit. I was working in Dallas at the time and had a terribly low credit score. It was tough to get a loan for a Mercedes. I was making decent money, but not great money. I couldn't afford a Benz, even the entry-level one I had my eye on. But I was determined. I visited a handful of dealerships and was turned down time and again. I finally found a car lot that had a pre-owned model. They charged me 13 percent interest and allowed me to make the down payment in two installments.

You get the picture. I wanted this car to impress people. It was important to let them know I had "made it." It would be easy for me to take this story and twist the meaning into something like, "Persistence pays off. I got what I wanted." That may be true, but I did it for the wrong reasons.

The car was heavy and acceleration was slow. It drove nicely on the highway, though it was not necessarily a fun car to drive. But I relished it. Visits to the dealership for scheduled maintenance became social events and were always entertaining. They lay coffee and doughnuts out in the morning and would give me a courtesy ride to work. I was treated like someone special at the Mercedes dealership and I needed to be special.

I bought that car way too soon. It was a poor financial decision, but I'd wanted to own a Benz ever since leaving high school. This would let the world know I was successful at a young age. Stepping out of that car, I held my head higher and smiled more. It gave me confidence in the moment. I felt like the rich and famous. Was this how my wealthy aunt felt? I wondered. I didn't want it to stop. Years later, I would buy a second, third, and fourth Mercedes, and each time I would enjoy the attention I would get from people admiring my car.

New York City, where most people travel on foot or by subway, changed that for me. I wasn't able to impress people with my car when I walked to a restaurant or to see a Broadway show. No longer did I have a big fancy car that instantly radiated the message, "I'm a success!"

The insecurity returned. Once again I was a loser. So my lesson is—buy your fancy car when you can afford it. Enjoy it and feel good about the compliments, but do it for yourself and do it on your own time. Run your own race.

People Need People

Tapping into your inner greatness also requires other people. For years, I thought I had achieved everything on my own. I was a self-made man.

Nothing could have been further from the truth. We need others in our lives for us to succeed. I needed a station manager to take a chance and hire me in high school. I needed engineers to make the broadcasts sound great. And most of all, I needed Stan Bunger.

Stan is one of the best radio broadcasters I know. He sounds smooth, relaxed, and as friendly as your next-door neighbor when he reads the news. Stan was the first newscaster I had ever heard who had a non-announcer style. I was impressed and knew immediately I wanted to be like Stan. I asked him to critique my on-air performance and he graciously agreed. I wanted to hear the full critique—all the bad stuff.

By broadcast standards, my voice was never very deep. My mid-range pitch was very average. I had even considered smoking just to make my voice deeper and a little raspier. I'm glad that was only a passing thought!

When Stan offered his critique, I remember thinking he wasn't hard enough on me. He told me my delivery was fine and that I just needed to be myself—not easy words to absorb and understand. Being myself, I thought, meant being the shy, insecure guy I had always been, and nobody wants that.

But his advice advanced my career. I realized what Stan meant when I took a job at a competing radio station. It was the first all-news FM station in Dallas. The staff was excited at the prospect of a news format on the FM dial, for news had always been relegated to AM radio.

My boss was Peter Gardner, one of the nicest guys in the business. His advice upon my arrival was very similar to Stan's: be yourself. Peter explained that I had a pleasant personality and that I should let that be heard on-air. My career changed at that moment. And, for a while, I wasn't sure it was for the better.

The change in my delivery also brought about my first listener complaint (that I knew of, anyway). I was devastated by it. But my co-worker, Suzanne Calvin, explained to me that this was good news. "You see," she said, "this means you are making a difference." Suzanne went on to explain that no complaints meant listeners had no opinions—I wasn't making a difference.

Over time, I received many more compliments and very few complaints. Thanks to Stan and Peter's advice, and some comforting from Suzanne, my career advanced.

Sometimes we need people to teach us other sorts of lessons, which brings me to radio station manager Bob Donns. He was a very smart guy, but we did not hit it off. His program director hired me at the station, which for one reason or another could not hang on to a news director. I arrived from Austin where I'd been covering the Texas capital and carrying out general assignments for a radio station there.

From time to time, Bob questioned my news judgment. He would ask why he had heard a story on another station but not ours. I usually fired back that I had aired three stories the other station hadn't touched. But Bob was not pleased with my defensive nature.

I let it be known I had worked in larger markets and I knew what I was doing. Deep down, I was scared to death I would miss a story, so I used my attitude to cover this up. Bob and I butted heads constantly for the year and three months I was on the job.

One day, Bob called the news department (me and my only reporter, Patty) into his office. He informed us that the receptionist had just taken a message from US Senator Phil Gramm's office. They wanted to send us a pre-recorded sound bite from the senator.

Bob wanted to follow up. I told him that we had not taken the feed and that it was no big deal. Lawmakers constantly recorded messages and had interns call local radio stations to feed the audio. This was essentially a PR campaign for elected officials. Bob was furious, screaming that he didn't want to receive a call from the senator himself, inquiring about the sound bite.

Once again, I told Bob it was no big deal and that Senator Gramm would not be calling him because he had much more important things to do than speak with the general manager of a small market radio station.

Bob shouted, "I ought to fire both of you and start from scratch!"

I responded, "That's your choice."

He became even angrier. "Get out of my office!"

My response just incensed him more. "I'll leave, but not before you calm down. You're going to have a heart attack."

He fired back, "God dammit, get out!"

This is a perfect example of what not to do.

Bob was very hard on me and for no good reason. I believe this even today. But I handled it all wrong. I could have acknowledged his criticism and moved on. I could have been less antagonistic. Instead, I spent a year and a half being miserable at that radio station.

After leaving, I learned a valuable lesson. I realized I would not win when it came to a disagreement with my boss and that a more diplomatic approach would have made life easier for me. But I needed this unpleasant experience to teach me that.

Sometimes the people who help shape us can be adversaries, which is why it's so important to have mentors. I had Stan Bunger. I also had Scott Martin. Nobody has given me more solid advice in my career.

Scott is a successful radio guy who's been everything from a disc jockey and a program director to talk show host and news guy. He's a very talented broadcaster and has a delivery not all that different from Stan's and mine. With a guy-next-door approach to his craft, it was natural for me to warm up to Scott.

I first met him in Austin, Texas, in 1991. He had just been hired for an afternoon disc jockey shift at the station where I was working. Scott had a great personality and people were naturally drawn to him. I sought out his advice and he was eager to share. Any time I had a problem, I consulted Scott for his wise counsel. Had it not been for him, I never would have got through the rough times with Bob Donns.

Scott taught me how to deal with bosses effectively, making them feel good and making me look good. At one place of employment, I felt I was not making a salary on par with my coworkers. Scott suggested I ask my boss for a salary *adjustment* rather than a *raise*. He explained that the terminology would get the message across that I wasn't looking for a 2 or 3 percent raise, but a big jump in money instead. I followed the advice. My boss was clearly taken by surprise, but I ended up with the money I was looking to make.

Another great piece of advice for negotiating was to quickly state my desires and then shut up. Scott told me that nobody, including bosses, likes awkward silence. It was up to me to be tough and wait out the silence. Most of the time, we ask for a raise, and then the room falls silent. We don't like the awkwardness of the moment, so we start talking. And in doing so, we talk ourselves out of the raise. We say something like, "I know times are tough and the company is looking for ways to save but I believe I deserve a raise."

You may be thinking, "What's wrong with that approach?" Sounds pretty good, right? Guess how your boss is going to respond? He'll use your words against you by saying, "Times *are* tough, and the company is looking to save money. I wish there was something I could do, but there isn't." See how fast that can turn around? If you remain silent, your boss will start talking and may not have a good reason why you can't have the raise.

Another gem from Scott's collection is the "walk the deal" approach. This has come in handy every time I buy a car (and I've purchased a lot of them). When the salesman says he's making his best offer, you thank him for his time and start to walk out the door. The last thing he wants is for you to walk out and possibly head to another dealership. He'll do everything he can to keep you there. And he will almost always sweeten the deal.

This can also work with other types of negotiations, but a word of caution: you must be willing to walk out empty-handed. There are occasions where this strategy just doesn't work, albeit rarely.

Discovering your inner greatness is simple. Be authentic, do what feels right, and take advice from those who are positive and eager to help. They will help you tap into your inner greatness if you let them. It's determination, passion, and a willingness to stick it out that translates into success.

Lesson:

1. Tap into your inner greatness. Find your skills and your passion and use them to your advantage.
2. Realize those who are famous and successful are not all that different from you and me.
3. Seek out mentors—those who have been successful can point you in the right direction.

CHAPTER 5

The Perception of Success

Donald Trump, Oprah Winfrey, Bill Gates—names synonymous with success.

Money, fame, and power are arguably the key definitions of success. Just one of those qualities will do—having all three is the ultimate sign of success. And there is tremendous pressure for us to achieve these societal standards, even if this isn't something we desire.

There's nothing wrong with achieving money, fame, or power, but these criteria are just about the only factors on which success is based. Because of this, many people who felt inferior as children base their goals on one of these three factors and continue to feel like failures until they achieve the set goal.

I should know. This is how I spent the greater part of my life. As an extremely introverted child, I had yearned to be liked and, to me, that equated with achieving success. Successful people were loved the world over, and I wanted to be one of them.

As a result of my misguided thinking, I overachieved. I based my self-worth on my career and bank account. A bad day at the office was devastating for me. If I made mistakes, I thought it meant I was a bad person. A great day at work put me in a state of euphoria.

What's worse is that the responses I got led me to believe I was doing it the right way. During my junior year of high school we moved from the Republic of Panama to Altus, Oklahoma. It was tough to make friends, but on the first or second day of class, a boy named Brent McKnight approached me, and we became instant friends.

Outside of Brent, nobody in that school knew my name. I never spoke to anyone unless I was spoken to. I felt afraid to approach my classmates because they might reject me. I would rather be alone than face rejection. They say the opposite of love is not hate but indifference, and that's what I felt in my junior year. Kids didn't make fun of me as in previous years; they simply ignored me. It was as if they didn't know I even existed.

I believed my only hope of changing this was to become a celebrity, and in small-town Oklahoma that meant a job at the local radio station. And that's exactly what happened. I was hired during the summer, and my senior year was like no other in my educational career.

Pursuing that first job in radio was one of the bravest endeavors of my life up to that point. After deciding broadcasting would be my career, I recorded myself onto a cassette tape, pretending to be a disc jockey and a news reader. I mailed this tape and a rather sparse résumé to KWHW radio—the only radio station in the city of Altus, Oklahoma. When I called to follow up, the general manager said he had no positions open and did not believe there would be any for the foreseeable future. I felt let down, but I knew it was a long shot for a high school kid with no experience to get the job in the first place.

A few months after this rejection, I read in the local paper that the radio station had been sold and there was a new manager on board. Every day after school I would drive down Cypress Street, staring at the radio studio and dreaming of the day I would work there. Sometimes I'd even park my car across the street in the evening and just gaze into the window. I'm amazed nobody called the police to report a suspicious vehicle every night.

I knew the only way to get the job I wanted was to go in and ask for it. So after psyching myself up over the course of several weeks, I entered the building with my tape and résumé in hand. Nelle Brown, the receptionist and copywriter, greeted me and asked if she could help. "I'd like to see the general manager," I said. She asked why and I told her I was there about a job.

A kind man named Jimmy Young was the new manager at the station and he agreed to see me. I told him I would sweep the floors, take out the trash, and answer the phones . . . and that I would do it all for free. I told Jimmy this was going to be my career and I needed to learn the business. He told me whatever work I did I would get paid for it, and that he would be in touch.

About a week later my mom had sent me to the store with my older sister, Angie, to fetch some items for dinner. As I pulled up to the house, my mother and little sister were standing outside shouting, "KWHW called!" I had a watermelon in my hand and nearly dropped it. I was shaking, but I dialed the phone and got a hold of Dave Madl, the program director at the radio station.

He offered me a weekend job running syndicated programming and doing a live weather report once an hour. I was so excited I was jumping up and down while trying to remain calm on the phone. I'll never forget that day. A dream came true for me because I put myself forward.

Getting that job proved to be a rush at school as well. When I returned to class, I was greeted in the hallways. Everybody knew who I was even though I didn't know them. They had heard me on the radio. They gossiped about the kid on the radio—and I loved it!

I was never involved in sports and felt I couldn't relate to the jocks in school, but lo and behold, members of the football and basketball teams were also saying "hi" in the hallways between classes. I was mesmerized by this newfound fame and attention. I craved more of it. It was like a drug and I was addicted, chasing the high.

It didn't last long. It would be years before I would realize that a job can't fulfill a person. Money can't do it either. And the same can be said for fame.

A great job, full bank account, and a little notoriety can be wonderful, but they should only be used to enhance your life. Not *become* your life.

Defining Success

My friends and I were languishing in huge, plush sofas at the luxurious Langham Huntington Pasadena hotel after enjoying a magnificent dinner. We wanted to enjoy the live music from the bar and at the same time share in some interesting conversation.

Someone posed the question: who was more successful—Steve Jobs or Bill Gates? In the ensuing debate, figures of their amassed wealth were tossed around, but I wasn't falling for such a simplistic definition of success. I argued that each was successful in his own right. Each had accomplished his desired goals—or, in the case of Jobs, as many goals as time would allow.

Bill Gates, as co-founder of Microsoft, had brought computer ease to the masses through basic computing functions. Virtually every PC in the world today runs on Windows. Jobs was an innovator. Whilst his Apple products may not have been a staple of every household, his iPhone was the template upon which all other smartphones are based. Both men were passionate about technology. Both were extremely successful and amassed billions of dollars in wealth. And there lies our lesson.

We've been taught that success depends on how much you have in your bank account, what kind of car you drive, the size of your house, or how famous you are. Society's definition of success is limiting and puts undue stress on all of us to achieve and accumulate more. If we don't meet the set standard, we feel inadequate. Parents encourage their children to become doctors or lawyers, not for the purpose of helping others, but to earn a big paycheck.

Don't get me wrong; there's absolutely nothing the matter with someone who achieves great things or amasses a huge bank account. But if this does not appeal to you, go your own way, set your own goals, and don't worry about what people think.

My mother has said to me that she feels she hasn't accomplished much in her life. I constantly remind her that she raised three children, none of whom was ever thrown in jail or ever had a drug problem. We're all productive citizens who are compassionate toward others. What more could a mother ask for from her kids?

As Mom gets older and starts to take inventory of her life, she worries that she hasn't left a mark. And she couldn't be more wrong. She stood by my father throughout his entire military career, encouraging him as he took on new assignments and challenges. She attended formal balls held by the military brass. She sat in the bleachers as my father coached his squadron's softball team. And she provided stability in our household by making sure dinner was served every night at five p.m. and that everybody had a chance to talk about their day across the dinner table.

When I applied for my first job in radio, my mother secretly worried that they wouldn't hire me because I lacked experience. She called the radio station and asked the program director to please "let my son down easy," adding, "He has his heart set on this job." Luckily for me, Dave Madl told my mother she need not worry because he was thinking about hiring me anyway. And he did.

Mom called out of love. She's always looked out for her children.

When I was in the third grade, some neighborhood bully stole my bag of candy on Halloween. I ran back home, crying. My Mom flew out of the door, dragging me along the street, until we found the kid. She grabbed his bag and dumped it into mine, and we went back home. She was my hero that night.

Early in my career, paychecks didn't last until the next payday. I was always short of cash. But it never failed that I'd go to the mailbox a few days before the pay period ended and there would be a card from Mom with a twenty-dollar bill inside. She always wrote something encouraging to put a smile on my face. I so desperately needed that money, and Mom knew it.

I have so many similar stories, as do my sisters. Our mother is the best, and we all know how lucky we are to have her in our lives. To me, Diana Wheelis has been extremely successful. Not all women can be great mothers or great wives, and my mom is both.

My sister Amy is another example of success. She never wanted a career, but instead wanted to be a housewife and mother. Perhaps this was because she had a great mentor in my mother. Amy married a wonderful man and had two girls whom I adore. She has dinner on the table every night when my brother-in-law Ron gets home. A self-taught gourmet cook, Amy has an amazing talent for cooking and baking. In the first years of their marriage, Ron put on several pounds. He eventually took up marathon running to keep the weight off.

Amy was always passionate about being a homeroom mother, baking goodies to take to the girls' school. They would make crafts and gift bags for students during all the holidays. And don't think she's a pushover who answers to her husband. Amy runs the household and admits herself that she can be a bit bossy. But why should she bow to societal pressure and try to pursue a career when she loves being a full-time wife and mother? This is my idea of success: defining what you want in life and going for it.

A few years ago Amy helped out some friends at their business and enjoyed it so much that she decided to work outside the home on a part-time basis. Notice here that her goals changed a little. That's encouraged! Whatever you decide to do early on, you always reserve the right to change your mind as you go.

When I was a teenager and realized I wanted to be in broadcasting, I told my mother that one day I would be the highest-paid TV news anchor. I followed a career path believing I would get there eventually. When I broke into television, the teenage dream was still a goal of mine.

Then I discovered I didn't care for TV as much as I enjoyed radio, which I felt was more intimate. I had more control over what I would say and how I would say it on the radio. There weren't a ton of producers and editors hacking away at my scripts. I changed my goal and sought to be the best radio news anchor I could be.

It's okay to change goals. I don't feel like a failure because I didn't become the highest-paid anchor on TV. In fact, that goal was set for the wrong reasons to begin with. I only wanted to be the "highest paid" because that's what I thought success was at the time!

Stop Pursuing the Happy Life

We might also look at happiness as success. This is probably the only self-help book that will tell you a happy life is impossible. Do not despair—happiness can be achieved, but a happy *life* will elude you forever.

I have some explaining to do.

Happiness is an emotion, just like anger, fear, or sorrow. And we need all of these emotions to cope with life. Unfortunately, we have all grown up with common misperceptions: that lots of money, a Prince Charming, an attractive woman, or perfect job will lead to "happily ever after."

For years, we saw movie stars depicted as glamorous, rich, and happy. But with today's information flowing twenty-four hours on the Internet, celebrities can no longer manage their images. And what a revelation! The likes of Lindsay Lohan, Charlie Sheen, and others who have plunged themselves into hot water show that money and fame cannot guarantee happiness.

What you are looking for is fulfillment. Most folks don't realize this, so they continue pursuing anything they think will make them happy. The crash of the housing market is one key example. We thought buying a bigger house and impressing friends would make us happy. It only drove us deeper into debt and, when the interest rate adjusted, we realized we couldn't afford the four-thousand-square-foot home after all.

There was a time when the sighting of a Mercedes-Benz or BMW outside of New York or Los Angeles was a rare occurrence. Today, these cars are all over the place because everybody wants to be somebody.

The Perception of Success

If we truly reach fulfillment in our lives, we're bound to experience a lot of joy and happiness. So that's our goal: fulfillment. When you are fulfilled, you will still experience sorrow and perhaps anger from time to time. That's natural and totally human. Word of a dying loved one, for example, is sure to conjure sadness. And this is why the happy life is impossible. It's okay to express these other emotions. What's not okay is to dwell on them. For instance, when a person feels fulfilled, he or she will naturally spend some time grieving over a loss, but then be able to resume life as usual.

So how do we achieve fulfillment? Simply by making a single choice, and then another, and then another.

First, make a decision that you are worthy just the way you are. Accept yourself. This may seem difficult at first, but that's okay. Take it one step at a time. If you find things you don't like about yourself, consider changing them.

When I decided to start making changes, I didn't like the guy I saw in the mirror each morning. I believed I was selfish, demanding, and controlling. These were attributes that I knew had to change or I would not attract people into my life. And life is about people. I needed friends who respected me and enjoyed my company. I wanted my family to think of me not as the brother or son who was always right and way too selfish, but as a loving, giving human being.

> Make a decision that you are worthy just the way you are. Accept yourself.

Don't be confused. You are, in your core, a great human being. You need to accept that you are perfect, whole, and complete. However, we develop habits and ways of being that are not indicative of our true selves. It's perfectly fine to want to change our nasty habits. In fact, it's encouraged.

When I was in my late teens, I had purchased a new Mazda 626, my pride and joy. So every time my little sister asked to use my car because she didn't have one of her own, I would say no. It didn't matter that I didn't have plans to go anywhere. It was my car, and nobody else was going to drive it. Occasionally, my parents would force me to hand her the keys. I pouted the entire time she was gone.

One Saturday morning, my mother headed out for some errands. My parents were sharing one vehicle at the time, so sometimes my mom would jump in my car. I hollered downstairs, "Don't take my car!" Turns out Mom had a rough morning running these errands and had gotten into an argument with a manager at a store. When she arrived back home, I screamed, "Why did you take my car?" Mom was in tears—the only time I've ever said something mean enough to make her cry.

I felt bad afterward and thought to myself, this is *not* who I want to be. It would be years before I realized this wasn't me, not really. It was me being mean because I didn't like myself. The first step I took to change was as simple as saying, "I'm not going to be a selfish person anymore." There were times, after declaring that stance, that I found myself in situations where the selfishness was about to rear its ugly head. In those moments, I would stop, take a step back, and decide to be giving. In many cases, it takes a lot of practice to make a new habit or a way of living, but it will happen. Now I don't think about it. For the most part, I'm a giving person. After making the decision to change, I felt better about myself. I was on the way to being fulfilled.

Doing this over and over, with each and every attribute you wish to change, will result in a transformation—a fulfillment you never knew was possible. There is another aspect to fulfillment, and that is living the life you desire. It's tough to be fulfilled if you are in a job you don't like or if you are holding back your true self from

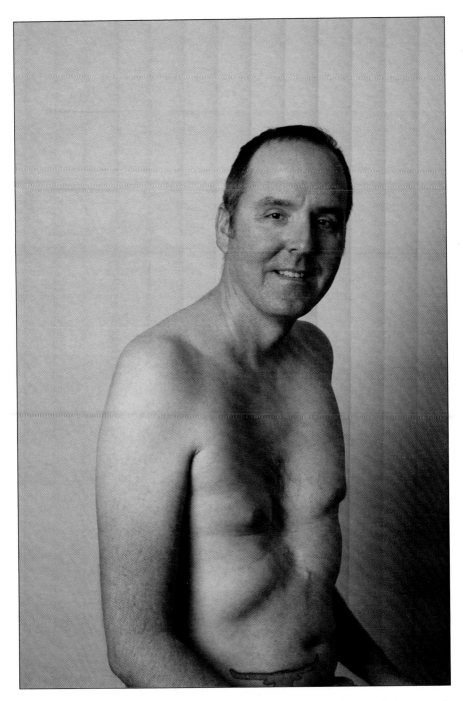

As an adult in my forties, years after a failed implant operation left me with the same crater in my chest and an added scar. 2012.

I sought out a job in television news to prove a guy with my condition could do it. 1999, KOKH-TV, Oklahoma City.

Junior high school. I was not only dealing with thick glasses, but also a concave chest.

On the beach in Panama. I refused to remove my shirt because I didn't want to expose my concave chest. 1983, Republic of Panama.

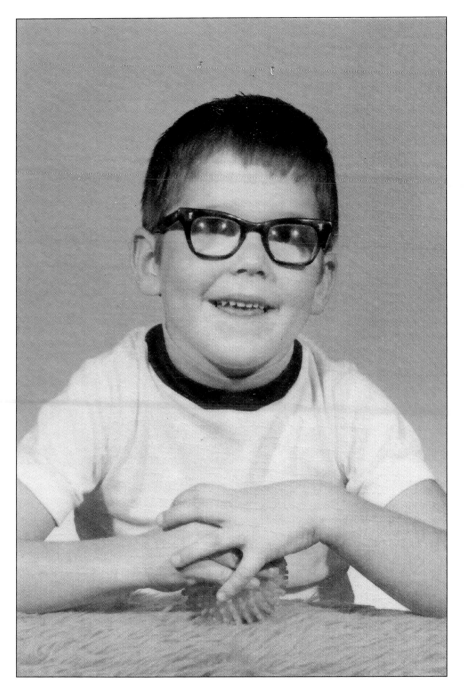

Kindergarten. I began my education wearing coke bottle glasses, for which I would be teased.

While in high school, I got my first job in broadcasting and was immediately popular in school. 1984, KWHW-AM, Altus, Oklahoma.

The two most influential people in my life: my parents.

Appearing on network television was the pinnacle of my career.

others. Don't live your life for somebody else. Choose a career path that works for you, not because you are trying to please others. We spend so much of our time working that it's important to find something you are passionate about.

There are far too many people who are doctors or lawyers because they were encouraged by their parents to pursue one of the career fields. Mom and Dad mean well. They want their kid to have a prestigious job with a great income. But what do *you* want? Sometimes we head down a career path because it's easy, or because we think it's what we want to do. Then years down the road we realize this isn't what we want at all.

My friend, Jeremy, is a perfect example of this. He's a wonderful and successful broadcaster, having worked in radio for years. But Jeremy really wanted to be an actor. At one point he did some community theater and loved it. But he goes to work every day with dread. There are a lot of people who would love to have Jeremy's job and his success, and he is grateful for what he has, but it's not his passion.

Now Jeremy feels trapped. He's been doing this job for so long and feels comfortable and secure. He doesn't want to throw that away by taking a chance in Hollywood. I'm not about to suggest that Jeremy or anyone else suddenly leave his or her job to embark on a childhood dream. Sometimes there are family obligations, bills to pay, and commitments.

But in Jeremy's case, he has no family to take care of and no debt. Plus, the guy has a sizeable savings account. His argument is that there are a lot of people who want to be movie stars and most of them are waiting tables in LA restaurants. He feels he's a little too heavy now and looking a bit old. My argument is that movies and TV shows feature people of all ages and types. In fact, an "ordinary-looking" man might get a number of roles, even if they're smaller roles with fewer lines. It can be steady work.

Taking a chance and seeing what's out there can be another step toward fulfillment. As I've said, a career is only one aspect of fulfillment. To achieve this is to make a well-rounded life. You need a career you are passionate about and you need people in your life to love. That's the second element of fulfillment.

Having been lucky enough to live in exotic places like Panama and small cities like Waco, Texas, I can tell you that people make the difference. Many of my friends are surprised I enjoyed my time in Waco. But they shouldn't be. I was surrounded by a great group of people. I was working at KCEN-TV. None of us was making much money at the time so we were all in the same boat financially. We went to happy hour on Fridays, consuming cheap drinks and sharing lots of laughs. I will never forget these moments.

When people ask me why I love Los Angeles so much, I tell them the weather can't be beaten. But I follow that with, "I have met the most wonderful people here." My friends are my family. And whether we are seeing a movie, having a long dinner, or just hanging out at someone's home, we enjoy our time together.

The third element of fulfillment is giving. This is simple and so rewarding. You can give money to a charity or to a man or woman begging on the street or you can give your time. Giving can take your mind off the stressful things in life. It moves the focus away from you and toward another human being.

I choose about three charities each year to donate to. I simply write a check sometime during the year to help out these worthy causes. In addition, I tend to give money to those who ask me for it when I'm at the post office or stepping out of my car at the store. Some people have told me it's not good to give to these people. "They'll only spend it on booze," they say. I give to them because they are in need. And if I were in their shoes, I might want to drown my sorrow in a drink as well. I'm not condoning the behavior and would prefer they use my money and other donations to get a hot meal, but I can't make that decision for them.

You can give of your time by building a house with Habitat for Humanity or volunteering at a local shelter. Another way to give is by being a mentor. This doesn't have to be an elaborate endeavor organized through a mentoring program. It can be as simple as you setting a good example for a young person. Be there to answer questions and help motivate this young man or woman.

One of the things I like to do is help those who want to become broadcasters. Sometimes I watch and listen to their demo reels and offer critiques and advice.

A college student named Brendon Geoffrion wrote to me asking for such advice. When he relocated to Los Angeles, I gave him some tips for getting into the radio business here. Within weeks, he had a job at a local station. Brendon aspires to be the next Ryan Seacrest, a radio and TV star. So when I had a red carpet event in Beverly Hills, I took Brendon along and allowed him to question some of the stars as they made their way down the carpet. This gave him experience and an opportunity to see how these media events are handled.

There are many people who've been in broadcasting a while who also ask for critiques and advice for moving ahead in the business. I'm always happy to oblige. You don't have to be a professional to be a mentor. By simply being a responsible adult, you are a positive influence on young people.

So remember, there is no happy life, but there is fulfillment. Live the life you want. Choose a career path through your passion, embrace friendship, and give back to your community.

Lesson:

1. Define success your own way, not by society's standards.
2. Money, power, and fame are fine, but realize success is not limited to these three factors.
3. Stop chasing happiness. Only fulfillment will bring about satisfaction.

CHAPTER 6

Famous and Flawless?

We've established that the rich and famous were just like you and me growing up. Their childhoods were not unlike yours or mine, give or take some circumstances. But surely the fame and money have changed the way they think about themselves? Not necessarily so. Even when professional success is reached, many people still have self-doubt. They see themselves as the insecure children they were growing up. You see them in the movies and on the red carpet in Hollywood. They live in gargantuan mansions and have more money than they will ever need. But life isn't always rosy for celebrities.

Angelina Jolie has said, "I struggle with low self-esteem all the time! I think everyone does. I have so much wrong with me, it's unbelievable!" I think it's unbelievable that someone so successful has so much self-doubt and is so critical of herself.

Whoopi Goldberg thinks it comes with the territory. "For some reason, all artists have self-esteem issues."

Singer James Taylor agrees, adding, "I think most musicians suffer from low self-esteem to some extent." The baggage we carry is no different for celebrities, which is why some act out in terrible ways.

Naomi Campbell, the strikingly beautiful supermodel, seemingly has it all. But behind the beauty, something was terribly wrong. Back in 2007, Campbell pleaded guilty to assaulting her maid. This apparently wasn't a one-time deal; she had been accused many times of abusing the help. Campbell is quoted as saying, "Anger is a manifestation of a deeper issue . . . and that, for me, is based on insecurity, self-esteem, and loneliness."

For other artists, the expression isn't outward anger and abuse, but escape through drugs.

Actress Demi Moore went through the wringer when she split with Ashton Kutcher and then entered rehab. Judging from an interview she gave to *Harper's Bazaar*, it appears that many of her problems stem from her low sense of self-worth. "What scares me is that I'm going to ultimately find out at the end of my life that I'm really not lovable, that I'm not worthy of being loved," she told the magazine.

Some actors and actresses pursue this career for the craft; others seek out the fame and approval of fans. This is like a drug itself. The celeb gets a high from the adoration, but it's short-lived because they don't truly believe they are worthy. This thinking can lead to very unhealthy relationships.

Oscar-winning actress Halle Berry has been the victim of domestic violence. She came from an abusive home and has said she chose to date men who were just like her father. In a 2010 interview with CNN, Berry said, "I think I've spent my adult life dealing with the sense of low self-esteem that is sort of implanted in me," adding that it came from seeing her mother abused when she was a youngster. "Before I'm Halle Berry, I'm little Halle who was a little girl growing in this environment that damaged me in some ways, and I've spent my adult life trying to really heal from that."

Unfortunately, these stories are not all that uncommon in show business. Hollywood grand dame Elizabeth Taylor held nothing back in her book *Elizabeth Takes Off.* "One of the dangers of growing up in Hollywood is that people tend to confuse 'image' with 'self-image.' Image refers to our appearance. Self-image deals with who we really are. Hollywood is filled with thin, beautiful women who are unhappy and unfulfilled, with little sense of self-esteem." Taylor noted her battle with weight, writing, "The large amounts of food I ate were a substitute for everything I felt I was lacking in my life. But what was really starving was my self-esteem and all the food in the world couldn't bolster it."

When I set out to write this book, I wanted to include some male celebrities who've battled insecurity and self-image issues. To my surprise, there were very few articles or books with famous men dishing out details of their innermost feelings.

Actors might feel they need to be strong to match the images we so often see on-screen. Talking about feelings, in their minds, could make them appear vulnerable or weak. I believe we need to hear from these guys who have questioned their worthiness. Obviously, over the years we've seen male celebrities battle weight issues or wear hairpieces. But other than a joke or two about this, the real, raw feelings are never shared. Are they afraid they won't get leading man roles if they appear vulnerable? Perhaps.

It could also be the differences between the sexes. On the whole, women tend to be more vocal about how they're feeling while men tend to keep everything bottled up. Many men believe that if they feel a certain way they need to *do* something to change it. Women feel they need to *share* it with others. I'm a fan of the latter. When we share our feelings, we let others know they aren't alone. It can help them avoid our pitfalls or, at the very least, provide a support system for us.

Oftentimes insecurity is the driving force behind the fame. Those who are insecure are seeking reassurance, so they are driven to succeed so they can ring up accolades. Again, this is short-lived, so after achieving fame, great reviews, lots of fan mail, and even an Oscar, they seek more. And they will always seek out validation from other sources until they deal with their own feelings and truly believe they are worthy.

Notable But Newsworthy?

The late Peter Jennings made it to the national anchor desk at a very young age. In his book *Peter Jennings: A Reporter's Life*, he pointed out he had been the youngest person ever to hold the job. Jennings admitted he got the position based on how he looked and the sound of his voice rather than his journalistic skills. Because of poor ratings, Jennings lost the ABC News anchor chair, only to return many years later. "Boy, did it hurt. . . . I felt like an outcast, assigned to the category of failure," Jennings wrote. He added that the moment of failure "was also a golden opportunity" because he was "obliged to figure out who I was and what I really wanted to be."

But Jennings, even after earning his credibility and going back, maintained some self-doubt. Because he was a high school dropout and didn't obtain a college degree, Jennings didn't feel he stacked up against his competition early on. It took years of reporting and self-education before he finally felt he had earned his position. He was one of the evening anchors on the big three networks, and yet there was that voice in his head suggesting he wasn't quite as well read as his competition. That may seem hard for people to believe or even understand. But if you are suffering from major self-doubt, think about how much more doubt you may experience if given a big promotion. There is immense pressure to do well along with the knowledge that your level of education is below that of your colleagues.

I know this all too well. As I mentioned earlier, for many years I felt inadequate in the news business because I hadn't completed college. It took decades and lots of reporting for me to feel confident in the role of a journalist. Even when I won a national award for Best Newscast back in 1995, I felt that I didn't deserve it or was living a lie as a journalist. Truth is, I earned that award and I deserved it.

In 2013, I had the good fortune of winning the prestigious Edward R. Murrow Award for my political reporting during the 2012 presidential campaign. Receiving this award marked the first time I accepted such an accolade at face value. I knew that I had put in the work and the product was worthy of such an honor.

Talk of this award and my political reporting brings me to Sarah Palin. My story here is not about politics, but resilience. Think whatever you want about Palin, but she's one tough cookie. The former Alaska governor took a beating in the media when she became John McCain's vice presidential running mate.

I remember being in the newsroom when Palin was introduced, along with her family, at the Republican National Convention. The governor has a son with Down syndrome. I was shocked beyond words when a female coworker of mine expressed her disdain of Palin, exclaiming, "That woman needs to be at home caring for that child!" Having a child with a handicap does not sentence one to a life as an inbound caregiver, not in my opinion anyway. Keep in mind that Palin doesn't necessarily see her son Trig's condition as a handicap or an imperfection, and I admire her for this.

In her 2009 book *Going Rogue: An American Life,* Palin spoke about Trig, her youngest child. She knew before he was born that he would have Down's. Palin wrote, "In my research on Down syndrome, I learned that these special kids most often bring joy into their family's lives. While they had developmental challenges, they were also affectionate, generous, and cheerful." Palin said she wanted the family to know there was a purpose for this child and encouraged family members to refrain from focusing on the negative.

She penned a note from the perspective of God in *I Hope Like Heck: The Selected Poems of Sarah Palin*: "Some will think Trig should not be allowed to be born / Because they fear a Downs child won't be considered "perfect" / In your world. / (But tell me, / What do you earthlings consider 'perfect' / Or even 'normal' anyway? [. . .] Have you noticed I make 'em all shapes / And sizes?" Palin had empowered her family and this child even before his birth.

I watched an episode of *Sarah Palin's Alaska*, on the TLC network, in which she visited a relative who also had a child with Down syndrome. Palin choked up when talking about this child, as he was older than her son, Trig. The former governor noted how happy this kid was and what joy he brought to his family, and she could see that Trig would be following this same path, bringing her much joy.

Palin, often ridiculed for not being "smart enough," was brilliant in the way she handled the birth of her son. Parents can take a lesson from this. Instead of looking at a disease or a syndrome as a burden, rather concentrate on the goodness of the child. Don't get me wrong; children with such issues sometimes require more attention and care than their siblings who are disease free, and it can be exhausting. These parents are to be admired, and this further illustrates the strength of Sarah Palin.

Big Guys Fall Too

In the last several presidential election years, billionaire Donald Trump made headlines as a possible candidate—mostly as a third-party candidate. But leading up to the 2012 presidential bid, Trump was even considering a run as a Republican candidate. He too received a lot of criticism from the media. But the idea of running earned Donald Trump a lot of coverage, further building his brand.

Even a billionaire has his share of problems. Trump reflected on his financial crisis that occurred back in the late 1980s in his book, *Trump: How to Get Rich*. The Donald wrote that he lost focus. "I owed billions upon billions of dollars—$9.2 billion, to be exact. . . .That was the low point." He learned a lesson: All that is achieved can be lost. So today he works as hard as he did as a young developer in the '70s. Trump's advice: "Don't make the mistake I did. Stay focused."

Have you ever failed at something? It's one thing to learn from that mistake and move forward, but too many people become paralyzed by it. If they've failed in business, they go to work for someone else and will never take a chance on themselves again. A failure is a learning experience, not a judgment on your inability to complete a project. Donald Trump didn't allow his financial troubles to hold him back. He not only turned it around, he flourished!

Trump offers this advice to those pursuing their dreams: "Positive thoughts will create positive visuals. Have you ever heard someone say, 'I can just *see* it!' when they are enthusiastic about something?" Trump goes on to recommend that you keep a book of inspiring quotes nearby to reach for when negative thoughts start to enter the picture.

Singing to a Different Tune

One of the greatest lessons in life comes from Willie Nelson. The country singer essentially says you need to be you and not an image created by somebody else. Nelson recalls in his book *The Tao of Willie* that in the early 1960s, famous singers Faron Young and Patsy Cline had hits with songs he had written, but Nelson had little success as a singer himself. "I tried to fit in by looking the way they wanted me to look, and I just didn't look like me. I also tried to sound the way they wanted me to sound, and I didn't sound like me either." But he eventually decided to be himself. His famous braided hair earned him the nickname "the Red-headed Stranger." Any country music agent or executive would have argued that the look was not in step with the image of Nashville and would not go over with country fans. But since Nelson wasn't seeing much success under their guidance, he decided to just be himself on stage.

Willie stopped forcing his voice, and country fans embraced his sound. He also found record executives who believed in him. If you listen to some of his early recordings, you'll notice a marked difference in the way Nelson sings. Clearly when he's doing it in his own style, the songs sound more authentic, which is where he found his success.

Katy Perry's story is similar. The documentary *Part Of Me* points out that many record executives knew she had talent, but just didn't know what to do with her different sound. She'd be signed by a label and then dropped. Just being signed is a great achievement, but Perry was discouraged after being dropped. She didn't try to change her style because she believed in herself.

There seems to be something very genuine and authentic about Katy Perry. She's someone who is not concerned with having the thinnest waistline or becoming a flawless visual image. She told *Parade* magazine, ". . . I've realized that it's time for me to show my audience that you don't have to be perfect to achieve your dreams.

. . . I'm okay with having bad dance moves. I'm okay with having horrible lower teeth. That's what makes me me, and for some reason it's worked out all right." She eventually found a record label that embraced her sound and allowed her to work with great producers, and she started cranking out hits. She's a role model for young girls to pursue their dreams and not focus on self-perceived flaws.

Laugh It Off?

Comedian Kathy Griffin struggled with her self-image for years, and still does to some degree. In her autobiography *Official Book Club Selection: A Memoir According to Kathy Griffin*, she talks about bullying from her childhood. Griffin notes, "As a kid, I was ugly, I was freckly, I had short, wiry orange hair." One day her parents took Kathy and her brother horseback riding. The instructor said to her brother Johnny, "Let me get a smaller horse for your little brother." Griffin was horrified, started crying, and shouted, "I'm a girl. I'm a girl." The kids at school would call her a dog and bark at her.

Her school days were torture, but Kathy found an outlet—humor. And when *The Mary Tyler Moore Show* debuted, she found someone she could relate to in the character Rhoda. "When Rhoda burst through the door in her Gypsy headscarf [. . .] I was like 'Who is *that*?' Oh my God!" Griffin says she fell in love with the idea of being a sidekick, especially because Rhoda had all the jokes, many of which were self-deprecating. The character truly spoke to Kathy.

But years later, after success on the sitcom *Suddenly Susan* and her own show *Kathy Griffin: My Life on the D-list*, she was still fragile. During an appearance on NBC's *The Tonight Show*, host Jay Leno made a derogatory remark about her looks. When they went to commercial break, Griffin started crying. Leno apologized, and Griffin later said she just wasn't expecting that. All those memories of kids barking at her had surfaced again.

Kathy Griffin was very vocal about having plastic surgery. But even those procedures didn't cure her insecurities. She still viewed herself as unattractive, though she was seemingly quite happy with the improvements. Her outlet is humor, and oftentimes she's poking fun of others, but she spends a great deal of time also making fun of herself. This is not uncommon. I've known people with weight issues who do this. They call themselves names like "big boy" or talk about "my fat fanny." This can give the impression that they've accepted their weight and it's no longer an issue for them. Not so for those friends of mine. It's just their way of getting the "fatness" out in the open so nobody else can make fun of them. Sometimes it works and sometimes it doesn't. I've seen other friends pile on the fat jokes, thinking it's okay to chime in given the fact that the fat guy has poked fun at himself first.

This hits home for me as well. As I was preparing for this book, I asked a friend to do a photo shoot with me. I would be bare-chested. This is the first time I had ever posed for a picture showing off my concave chest. The object of the shoot was to highlight it, which meant we had to fiddle with the lighting and angles to properly illustrate how deep the hole was. I would be publishing the photo in this book, so it was important to get it right. I remember my friend behind the camera saying something along the lines of "Move to the right . . . yeah, show me that horrific chest." It was his way of lightening the mood and dealing with the awkwardness, but it hurt. I didn't say anything at the moment. We needed the photos and I did not want to stop the process.

I've been picked on and heard a lot of mean things about my chest, but it hurts the most when it comes from someone whom you like and trust. I don't fault my friend because he didn't know. Many people are unaware that this is uncomfortable or downright hurtful.

So after all these years and even after writing a self-help book, I still get hurt when a friend or family member pokes fun at my chest. The difference now is that I can deal with it. I don't shut down. I acknowledge the pain and move on. I now realize my value as a human being. I have many great qualities inside and out, and I steer my focus toward those things rather than dwell on the one thing. Take a lesson from those celebrities, some of whom have dealt successfully with their insecurities and others who are still struggling.

Lesson:

1. Know that money and fame won't solve your problems.
2. Know that you are worthy.
3. Even the rich and famous have setbacks, but they keep going. You should too.

CHAPTER 7

Be Powerful

One way to break through the Perception Myth is to realize the power that lies within each of us. When people are asked about their goals, they often say they want money, power, or fame . . . or all three. Often, one leads to another. A famous person has the power to reach millions; therefore, they can champion a cause and make a difference. Those with money can also be influential. That's why they give to political campaigns.

This chapter is about the power *you* possess—the power to get things done. It doesn't necessarily take money or fame; sometimes it's simply a matter of asking for what you want.

Many of us feel powerless in this world. Politicians are making decisions for us, and big money influences that decision-making. The rich get treated better at stores and restaurants. As a frequent gambler, I know that people who spend a certain amount in the casinos are comped rooms and shows and can even cut lines at the buffet. While money does talk in this world, never underestimate the power you hold by simply stating what you want.

Here's one powerful example: I took a course from Landmark Worldwide, a transformational program focusing on the way we look at ourselves. We were just a few days away from graduating when I had a revelation during the course and felt truly transformed. Landmark was instrumental in helping me accept my concave chest. They did it not by telling me it doesn't look bad or isn't a big deal, but by acknowledging the inward direction of my chest and explaining to me that I'm the one deciding that this deformity is a negative. While that may seem simple, I needed to hear it. I had always rejected therapists who tried to get me to focus on my other assets. This time they were telling me not to ignore the chest, and put it into perspective.

Some people might reject me because of the deformity, but that doesn't mean everybody will. In fact, people reject others because of the way their nose is shaped or even the color of their hair. Having a concave chest doesn't mean I'm out of the game, it just means I won't hit a home run with everyone, and it took Landmark to get me to this place.

After this breakthrough, I was so excited and wanted nothing more than for my mother to be there on the graduation night. The trouble is that my mom and dad live in Texas and I was in California. Oh, and my mother was deathly afraid of flying. There's no way she would be able to make it. On a Saturday I called Mom and told her about the progress I had made and that I understood she doesn't fly, but I wanted her to know nothing would mean more to me than her presence on Tuesday night. My mother said she would check and see what she could do. That's the typical answer you hear from people when they're not going to follow through with something, I thought. She just won't be there.

The next day, Mom called, saying that she had booked a flight and she and my younger sister would be there for graduation. I couldn't believe it! How was this possible? My mother does not fly. This is a woman who drove overnight, rather than fly, to be with my grandfather on his deathbed. She couldn't muster the courage to take a plane then, but here she was about to get on a jet simply because her son asked her to do so.

Before you decide something is impossible, why not try first?

This not only spoke of the power I never knew I had, but it was also a defining moment for my mother. Because of the pleasant experience in the air, my mom and dad later booked a flight and spent Christmas with me in Los Angeles. And when my father did some temporary work in Alaska, Mom took a flight by herself to visit. A month later she was on a plane to meet me in Las Vegas.

My request served my interest, but it gave freedom to my mother. She can now fly anywhere, anytime, and not worry about it. Had I not asked her to be with me at the Landmark event, she might not have ever tried to get on a plane again. Before you decide something is impossible, why not try first? Most of the time you have nothing to lose but much to gain.

Asking for What You Want

Here's another example of the power we hold by simply asking for something. Shortly after purchasing my Porsche, some friends and I planned to meet in Las Vegas. Getting the idea I enjoy gambling? Rather than taking a forty-nine-dollar, one-hour flight to Vegas, I wanted to drive. My little car needed to break free and the desert highway was the place to do it, I thought.

In order to avoid the heavy traffic, I left very early in the morning and made good time. To avoid self-incrimination, I won't mention my highest rate of speed as that German engine growled across the desert like a lion hunting down its prey. The ultimate feast would be in Vegas, I thought.

No sooner did I cross the Nevada state line than my eye caught the blue and red lights flashing in my rear view mirror. I'd been busted. The highway patrol was pulling me over. There's nothing quite like the fear of breaking the law and being caught in the act. The officer was matter-of-fact and was not in the mood to hear excuses, so I offered none. I accepted the ticket and headed for the lights of Las Vegas. Soon after, my friends had diverted my attention and I was no longer thinking about that expensive four-hundred-dollar ticket.

After I got back to LA, I had more time to think. Not only was the ticket expensive, but it would reflect badly on my driving record, so I wanted to do something about it. Going to court would mean missing a day of work, another long drive, and a chance I would lose. After all, I was guilty of speeding. I called the small town courthouse and asked if I could speak to the judge. The clerk was friendly and said the judge did not take these types of phone calls, but offered a suggestion: I could write the judge.

I spent some time carefully crafting a letter acknowledging my guilt and the reason behind my behavior and asked for leniency. Yes, I told the judge I was guilty. Notice I didn't try to lie about speeding, nor did I ask the judge to drop the ticket. I simply asked for leniency. I was prepared for everything from rejection to the dropping of the ticket.

When I asked a few friends and colleagues to look over my letter, they all agreed it was well written, witty, and sincere. But each of them warned me not to expect results. They told me how judges have heard every excuse in the book, and in essence, it was a waste of my time. Having nothing to lose, I decided to send the letter anyway.

Several weeks later, the court clerk called, telling me the judge had ruled on my case. The clerk said the ticket had been changed to a parking fine, reducing the amount I owed by hundreds of dollars. This would also mean the ticket would not appear on my driving record. What relief I felt. But there was also a sense of accomplishment and fulfillment. I had asked for something, knowing the odds were probably stacked against me, and my request was granted.

Notice that in both these examples, I was asking what most people would think was impossible. My mother had never planned to fly again. Judges have heard all the excuses and are tired of hearing them. Friends will tell you things are not possible because they have not pierced the Perception Myth. They're afraid to ask for what they want; therefore, they don't encourage others to take the risk.

Even when I decided to write this book, friends told me how difficult it was to get published. They rattled off lists: you're a first-time author, you're not a psychologist, and you're not a household name. All of that was true, but I knew I had a message that could help people and I believed in myself. I knew that someone else would believe in me as well.

Your friends want the best for you, so they caution you against taking risks. But without risk, there is very little gained.

I had been writing broadcast scripts for nearly thirty years, but that in no way was anything like writing a book. I didn't know where to begin or how to link chapters for a sense of flow. I hired an experienced and published author and editor to both edit my manuscript and educate me along the way. Then I reached out to a friend who had a connection to a literary agent and before I knew it, we were taking meetings with publishers. We had several offers and I couldn't believe it. Months before these meetings I had considered self-publishing and trying to peddle my book on my own. But by asking for help, I was able to find someone who could convince publishers I had a great message to share. Be bold and ask for what you want. You might just get it!

Missed Opportunities

And what if you decide not to ask? You may live to regret it. My friend John was working in Washington, D.C. and really wanted to get back to Texas to be closer to his family. I suggested he tell his employer of his desire to relocate and explain that he could do his job from any location. John argued it wouldn't work. "My boss wants everyone based in D.C.," he said. He was convinced there was no way his employer would give in. After all, if he let John move, he'd have to let everybody move and he wasn't about to do that.

"Are you sure about this?" I asked. "Perhaps he would make an exception." John ultimately decided it was best not to say anything. Mere weeks later, a fellow employee asked to move, which the boss considered. John eventually requested permission to move; his boss also took this under consideration and then made an offer to allow John to relocate.

This scenario could have turned out very differently. The boss may have decided to allow only one person to relocate and to keep everybody else in Washington. In delaying his request, my friend would have missed an opportunity.

Most of the time it's best to ask for what you want and let the boss or whoever tell you no rather than deciding it for them.

Don't get me wrong, your every request may not be granted. You should be prepared for rejection. But if you're asking for something you don't have and the answer is no, you haven't lost anything. You are in the same spot you were before you made the request.

However, if the answer is yes, you get what you wanted. You really have nothing to lose in this type of situation.

Use your best judgment when asking for something. In the news business, my employer put a blackout on vacation requests on 9/11. The thought was that terrorists may decide to mark the bombing anniversary with another attack and we would need all hands on deck for coverage. Obviously, in this situation, it wasn't wise to ask for time off. There are situations where you may not want to ask based on rules or guidelines your employer has imposed. But if those rules have not been set, ask and you may receive. Remember, there is power in direct communication.

Be Powerful. Be Vulnerable.

At the beginning of this book, I wrote about vulnerability and how I fought it for so many years. We're taught by our parents to be our best. Sometimes that translates into be *the* best. And when we feel we're falling short of being the best, we feel vulnerable. We don't want people to see our perceived shortcomings. So we pretend to have it together. We pretend to be without fault. And we put up walls so that people can't see into our lives and realize that we are human.

This was reinforced on the playground when we were children. As the new kid in town, you walk up to classmates and say, "Hey guys, what's up?" They, in turn, say something cruel because they don't want to be vulnerable. They're trying to be cool and you walk away feeling like a fool.

As adults, we see celebrities and politicians stumble and be ripped apart by the media. We're taught there is no room for error— no room for imperfection. It is okay to be vulnerable. In fact, University of Houston sociologist Brené Brown says it's critical to human connection. During her talk on TED.com, Brown said we are hardwired for connection. That's the human experience, yet some of us feel shame and fail to connect. Brown defines shame as fear of disconnection. Essentially, you hold back because you fear that if someone finds out about your secret, they will shun you.

This became apparent for me with friends who suffered from HIV and AIDS. In the early '90s, my friend George ended up in the hospital with an illness; doctors tested his blood and found out he had full-blown AIDS. George phoned me crying, saying he was scared to die. I was one of only a handful of people he told. Even some of his closest friends were kept out of the loop. There was a stigma and George didn't want to be a victim.

At his funeral less than two years after his diagnosis, his family kept the cause of death private. There were whispers, but nobody knew for sure how George died. The family was afraid of the stigma and felt ashamed. I thought at the time how difficult it must have been holding such a secret and living with the fear that someone would find out.

Before George's health forced him to quit his job, he was transferred to Oklahoma City. My parents were living there at the time and I asked them to show George around the city. They were happy to do it. I had shared George's condition with my parents, with his consent, because I needed emotional support handling his diagnosis.

Mom and Dad not only showed George the best places to live in the city, but they took him to dinner. They shared some appetizers, never flinching at the thought that George may have touched the food. Back then, people were still skittish, even those with the virus. In fact, George and I went out for drinks one night and I took a sip of his margarita. He was shocked. But being in the news business and covering the AIDS epidemic, I knew I would not get HIV from sharing a glass.

My parents were educated enough to know the sharing of an appetizer was okay too. George couldn't believe it. He thought my parents were the greatest. They knew about his AIDS, yet they shared food and exchanged hugs after dinner. I'm proud of my parents and their decision not to label George or avoid him in any way.

More recently, my friend Devon confided in me that he has HIV. His viral load is undetectable, as is the case with so many patients these days. HIV is no longer a guarantee of AIDS nor a death sentence. It's more of a chronic disease that can be treated with various drug cocktails.

Some of the stigma may have disappeared over the years, but the shame remains for many. Devon was diagnosed nearly seven years ago and has never told his family or any close friends, other than myself. There is fear his family will think he's failed in some way, that he hasn't lived up to their expectations as the perfect son with a wonderful job, great looks, and a promising future.

Devon and I did not know each other when he found out he was HIV positive, which meant nobody knew for many years. What a burden that must have been to carry alone: not being able to share your worry, fe   and concerns with another human being. Devon never got th   only a friend or family member could offer, all bec   o be judged.

This is   ocate for gay rights, yet there is shame ke   honest. I don't believe everyone who has   world, but when you are keeping it from al.   ere is a problem. Society is changing, people are less j.   about those afflicted with HIV, and I hope this will put an end   the shame.

I'm old enough to remember how divorce was a four-letter word at one time. During my childhood in the 1970s, kids who came from a broken home were outcasts. Single mothers were a foreign concept to my classmates. Children were looked down upon as second-class citizens. Even the adults had little to do with women and men who divorced. And I remember adults whispering as if the divorced spouses were somehow flawed because they couldn't keep a marriage together.

What a drastic change over the past several decades. Half the kids in any given class come from homes where the parents are divorced. There is no longer the stigma of being from a broken home. Society has realized that marriages don't always work out, but it doesn't mean the adults are bad people. In fact, divorce is probably healthy in many cases because the parents are no longer arguing in front of the children.

And we can't forget that kid with the Coke bottle glasses. I look back at pictures and somehow they seem cute. They certainly weren't at the time. But today, the term "four eyes" is rarely, if ever, used. So many children wear glasses that they're no longer a slim minority. Adults now purchase frames, without prescriptions, as a fashion accessory. Glasses are finally en vogue! Younger people are purchasing oversized frames so they can look nerdy, because that too is now "in."

For years I believed my biggest threat to my professional life was my sexuality. I hid in the closet until I was almost in my mid-twenties. I thought this would ruin my life. If people found out I was gay, they wouldn't treat me well. I wouldn't be able to have a job in broadcasting and follow my dreams, I thought. There were relatively few openly gay men in Hollywood or anywhere else in the public eye.

Because I was uneducated about homosexuality, I felt it was a flaw, and I couldn't bear to have another flaw. What would happen to that young man whose parents were so proud of him? I was so naïve and had never been around many gay people in my life. I thought they were all older men with mustaches and a lisp (not that there's anything wrong with that!). Intellectually, I should have known that there were many homosexuals in the world and that there had to be some my own age.

I was absolutely miserable with my life. I tried to date a few girls, but just couldn't. It didn't feel right. I knew I was gay. I had prayed for years for God to change me. I never sought out bars or any other places where gay men might hang out.

It wasn't until I met Tony Ramos that things changed. My younger sister and I were working retail together and she had a crush on Tony. A coworker told her to forget it because Tony was gay. I couldn't believe it! Tony was gay? But he looked so normal, I thought. Also, as far as I knew, he was the first gay person around my age who I'd ever met.

After mustering up enough courage, I approached Tony one day at work. I just said hello and asked him a few questions. He knew I was seeking him out as a gay man. My life changed that week. Tony took me to my first gay bar, showed me the ropes, and made sure I didn't get hooked up with the wrong people. I was so scared, but I had a buddy to hold my hand as I explored a new world. My relationship with Tony was never sexual. He was like a brother to me, and I love him to this day because of the gift he gave me: freedom to be myself.

The day I was supposed to go out to a gay bar for the first time, I sat my family down and came out of the closet. I could barely get out the words "I am gay" when I started bawling. My mom, dad, and little sister all cried too. My parents told me they loved me and all they desired was my happiness. But they did have some questions about all of this and wondered if it was just a phase. They asked that I see our preacher, and I agreed.

It was an uncomfortable meeting and even as I write this, there is still a bit of discomfort. He asked me what I was sexually drawn to and whether I admired boys' bodies in the locker room. I was quite frank with him, and he reported back to my parents that, indeed, their son was gay. I actually have him to thank, though I've forgotten his name. The preacher didn't try to change me or encourage my parents to do so. He told them I was gay and they should love me.

Despite the fact I told my parents I was gay, I kept it hidden from my coworkers. It was my big, dark secret. A few would find out, usually because I would befriend one of the women at work and they would ask me point-blank about my sexuality. Call it women's intuition, but they always knew. Well, most did. A few asked me out on dates and occasionally I'd go. At the end of the night, I would be a "gentleman" and give them a quick peck on the cheek. There would never be a second date with any of them.

It wasn't always rosy at the office. I was working in a small town in Texas, and when the general manager of the radio station found out I was gay, our relationship took a big turn for the worse. He had listened in on my phone conversations with my friend, Tony. That's how he found out.

During a staff meeting about our new health plan, my boss announced that we had a million-dollar cap, adding, "That ought to cover AIDS, Brad." I was mortified. First, I wasn't out to the rest of the staff and second, what a horrible thing to say! He was an asshole—you will encounter them in your lifetime. He thought I would quit, but I didn't. I didn't want to be without a job because that would have given him all the power. I waited until I was offered a good position elsewhere before I gave my notice. That was one of the most satisfying days of my life. In Texas, and many other states, it's perfectly legal to fire someone because they're gay, or say such horrific things to homosexuals. You may not condone homosexuality. You may have religious beliefs that conflict with it, but everyone should support laws to prevent employers from making such remarks. And think about this: if you fire people because they're gay, they'll be collecting unemployment—something you're helping fund anyway.

There was another "outing" that occurred at the office, with a far different outcome. I was hired as an anchor at Fox 25 TV in Oklahoma City, partly because I was a friend of the news director's wife. I'd like to think I was hired for my skills as well. Since she knew I was gay and had introduced me to the gay executive producer years earlier, he also knew about my sexuality.

The first day I arrived for work, Mike, the executive producer, told the staff that it was nice to have another gay man on the team, or something to that effect. I was stunned! This guy had just *outed* me in front of the staff. But it was also liberating. I had never really come out at any place of business before, but now everybody knew. I didn't have to worry about being found out.

Mike did me a favor. I was free to be me and live an authentic life. If someone asked me about a date, I didn't have to use generic pronouns to describe the guy I went out with the night before. I'm sure there were staff members who made fun of me behind my back, but they do that no matter who you are.

It's hard to describe the feeling of being absolutely authentic. When there are no lies, you don't have to worry about mixing up your story or having anxiety about a night out at a gay bar. This was one of the highlights of my career and mostly for personal reasons. I made real connections with coworkers. They got to know the real me without the walls that I had built at previous jobs. It was refreshing and true freedom.

I relay these two stories because they are opposite experiences. There's no telling how people will react if you tell them you're gay or they find out another way. Thank goodness society is changing and in many places it's not a big deal to have gay staff members. In fact, some places applaud it. But as I mentioned earlier, there are still areas of the country, namely the south, where you can be fired for being gay. That has to change. Nobody should be forced to hide their true identity in order to put food on the table. But don't think things are just fine in the bigger cities. There's another kind of subtle discrimination that takes place, and many women may relate. Again, times are changing, but for the most part there are more white straight men running corporate America than any other demographic. This means in order to really succeed and be included, you must be allowed in the old boys' club.

Even at the network level, this exists. I found it hard to get into that club because I didn't talk about sports or family or whatever else the straight managers chatted about. I found them cordial and professional, but they may have felt awkward speaking to me about personal issues because I was gay. Here's how it plays out. They like you, they promote you, but when it comes to plum assignments or other little perks, the straight guys win out.

A few years ago, ABC News moved its Los Angeles bureau to a new location. The television department was in charge of logistics because radio was such a small part of the bureau. Because I was an anchor, the manager in charge (a woman) assigned me the larger office among the radio crew. I was told this and shown the plans, but just before we moved in, someone in radio management (a straight white male) intervened and a reporter was given the bigger space. Keep in mind that I spent my entire day in that office with newscasts every half hour. My coworker was often on assignment outside the city or even the state. I could have used a little more elbow room.

So why the change? I can only surmise this was because my coworker was a member of the old boys' club. He spoke daily with management and they were tight. I adored my coworker, so I decided I would not try to fight that battle.

In 2008, I asked if I could cover at least one of the political conventions. Management told me I was needed on the anchor desk for consistency. Listeners were expecting me to anchor the newscasts every night, they told me. I bought it. My ego bought it. In 2012, the same manager asked me to fill in as a reporter while our L.A.-based correspondent attended one of the conventions. I suggested he stay on his beat in southern California and I go instead. That suggestion was rejected. Management attended the conventions, and this was a great opportunity for the boys to get together.

My political report, *Your Voice Your Vote,* won the prestigious national Edward R. Murrow award. So even without attending the conventions, I was able to produce an award-winning series. But it sure would have been nice to cover at least one of the conventions in the three presidential campaigns during my tenure at ABC. Not all discrimination is blatant and intended to offend or hurt. But when management excludes you or plays favorites with "the guys," it's unfair. I suspect many women feel this way. Even if you make it into management, you may not be included in the boys' club of off-color humor, ribbing, and outings, where relationships are forged beyond the office. These relationships often lead to major promotions down the road.

My message is this: no matter how people respond to you, continue to forge ahead. You'll get where you need to go, even if it's a little harder. Don't let any discrimination hold you back. Be authentic and be vulnerable because in the end, it will pay off. Even if people don't like one of your traits, they'll respect you for being yourself and being honest.

For so many years I had trouble with my sexuality in that I thought it could hurt me. I even found myself monitoring my behavior in public—making sure I did not offend. For example, in restaurants, some of my gay friends were loud and overtly feminine.

I detested that behavior, believing assimilation would win us more favor with the straight community. We needed to fit in with the straights, I thought.

I've since changed my position on this. I believe we should be ourselves, whether that's feminine, masculine, or somewhere in between. When we are authentic, we don't have to worry about being vulnerable because we are showing strength. So let your guard down, let people in, and be vulnerable.

Think about what you are holding back. What are you ashamed of and why can't you be vulnerable? When we show our vulnerabilities, whether it's our feelings or something about ourselves that we're not proud of, we run the risk of ridicule, but this is also a chance to get closer to people. We need to let others inside our inner circle and that takes vulnerability.

Researcher Brené Brown studied people who had a sense of worthiness. She found that those who felt this way had connection in their lives because they were authentic. Brown said, "They were willing to let go of who they thought they should be in order to be who they were." She added there was "a willingness to say 'I love you' first, the willingness to do something where there were no guarantees."

And here's something else she discovered: When you try to numb vulnerability, you get into trouble because you cannot selectively numb emotion. Brown noted, "You can't numb those hard feelings without numbing the other emotions" such as joy, gratitude, and happiness.

When you start being authentic and letting people get to know the real you, you become extremely powerful. The baggage you've been carrying is no longer a secret and can't be ammunition for your enemies, as so many of us fear. This doesn't mean you have to tell the world about your innermost feelings and secrets, but when you want to become closer to another person, honesty and vulnerability are key.

Lesson:

1. Decide what you want.
2. Ask for it and prepare yourself for the answer.
3. Get closer to people by being vulnerable.

CHAPTER 8

So You Had a Bad Day?

So you had a bad day? Let me guess, the clerk at the fast food restaurant was rude to you . . . and got your order wrong and you were late for work? The same thing has happened to me, but I didn't have a bad day.

How can we both experience the same events and yet be affected so differently? It's all about our perception. Sometimes it's a pretty easy task; other times you might find it a bit more challenging.

Your boss may have yelled at you for being late to work, but if you are a great employee, you were probably given a pass. Perhaps nobody said a word to you about your tardiness. If that's the case, there's no reason to be upset.

As for the rude clerk, perhaps he or she was under stress. The clerk may not have the knowledge you are about to learn in order to handle something stressful. The simplest way to deal with these kinds of things is to ask yourself, will I be thinking about this or even bothered by it a year from now? Chances are you won't be thinking about it a week from now. So get over it! Now!

It may in fact be worth following up with corporate or the manager of the restaurant if you feel this is something more than a clerk having a bad day. Otherwise, let it go and move on.

Now that you know you get to decide how your day is going to be, nobody else decides that from this day forward. Since we've all had bad days, try to be a little forgiving to a person who shows signs of stress. Perhaps compliment him or her to help change his or her mood. A little kindness goes a long way.

I was in Target around Christmastime and the clerk seemed very stressed. Not rude, but she looked exhausted and ready to leave. I simply said, "How are you doing today?"

She responded by saying, "Thank you so much for asking. Nobody has asked all day." It changed her attitude, and the customers behind me surely benefited from it.

Nancy found herself crying one morning after a visit with her grandson. Another argument between the two sent Nancy heading down the highway to Texas. This was one of many fights the two endured in their rocky yet loving relationship. Nancy was feeling sorry for herself. "Why was he so mean to me?" she asked herself. Tommy, the grandson, was surely asking similar questions.

For Nance, this was the beginning of a bad day. She was feeling sorry for herself and cried the whole way home. That's when she decided to stop by a local Indian casino. For Nancy, an avid gambler, the slot machines provide a place for her to forget the day's troubles and simply have fun. The decision paid off handily. Nancy won fifteen thousand dollars that night. Excited, she phoned Tommy to share the joy of her bounty. She couldn't believe she'd hit such a big jackpot. Suddenly, Nancy was preoccupied with the rush of winning rather than the depression of an argument with her grandson.

Let's make sure we're on the same page here. The jackpot does not negate the argument Nancy had with her grandson. I'm not suggesting one makes up for the other but that instead, our mindsets change as the day passes. This could have happened in the exact opposite order—a win, then an argument, and Nancy could have ended up angry and sad. The chances are that she would have handled the argument better after winning because she was in a better frame of mind. Nancy's day was neither good nor bad; it was simply her day.

This is the kind of mindset we need every day in our lives. Let's not classify our days from best to worst, but instead realize that there are many events that make up a day, which is all part of life.

When Nancy decided it was going to be a bad day based on the fight with the grandson, she did not see any good coming her way. How could she? We don't know what's coming down the pike. That's why we don't judge our day by one event or even two. What starts out with hiccups ends up with a windfall. Not bad.

> Let's not classify our days from best to worst, but instead realize that there are many events that make up a day, which is all part of life.

What's the Worst That Could Happen?

Have you ever expressed a desire to do something and have a friend tell you to go for it? They ask, "What's the worst that could happen?" I believe in taking risks, and I know a little something about the worst that can happen.

Back in 1988, I was asked to DJ a junior high school dance. I initially hesitated, but after some coaxing I obliged. The man who ran the DJ service had several "units" that he sent out, but he didn't have the manpower to cover all the gigs, so he asked me.

I had been in radio for four years by that point. I was used to speaking to large audiences, but only from my radio studio. I was terrified to go in front of people, especially these teenagers. You see, I never thought I had a great personality. Remember the shy kid with the Coke bottle glasses? That was the image I had of myself even though I was in radio and had ditched the glasses long ago.

On the radio, I had a mental script to go by. I would introduce the name of the record or read the weather forecast or a public service announcement. In front of these kids, I would have to convince them to get out on the dance floor and I wasn't sure I was hip enough to do so.

Off I went with my engineer to the dance in the small town of Pauls Valley, Oklahoma. And when we arrived we discovered we were short of music. Someone forgot to put a crate of albums in the van. I had little to play for the kids and most of the songs were older, not the current top forty.

I managed to find Bruce Springsteen's "Dancing in The Dark," which got the kids out on the dance floor. I followed up with "Shout"—a song prominently featured in the movie *Animal House*. The kids were excited and jamming. My DJ skills were paying off, or so I thought.

You've probably heard the song "Shout," but let me refresh your memory. The song has several false endings. That is, the singers and music stop, there's a beat pause, and then they resume singing. I knew that, or so I thought. When the first false ending came around, I sat at the DJ booth waiting for the song to resume. And then came the second false ending, at which time I started Bon Jovi's "You Give Love a Bad Name." Then the *Animal House* song resumed. I had two records going at the same time!

In unison, as if choreographed for a movie, the entire dance floor of teens turned toward my turntables and yelled, "What are you doing?" I can still remember all those angry faces staring at me as if I were some kind of idiot.

I was mortified, but quick on my feet. I turned on the microphone and said, "I was just checking to see if you were awake." I allowed "Shout" to continue to the end and then played Bon Jovi for the crowd. They were not happy campers. The dance couldn't end soon enough for me. I had just experienced the worst humiliation of my life. What could have been worse? I asked myself. I really wanted to just run out of the building and get away from it, but I couldn't. I had to stay and feel this humiliation for two more hours . . . two of the slowest hours of my life.

So, what did I glean from this experience? First, I know what it feels like to screw up in front of a large crowd. Don't get me wrong; it is a terrible feeling. Second, all these years later, it doesn't matter. I doubt if any of the kids, as adults, remember that night or the lousy DJ who performed. I certainly don't think about it much. I do occasionally bring up the story for a good laugh. And that's the lesson. I can now laugh about it. It's not the least bit traumatizing to me.

The Big Blooper

Life is complicated and we can face much more serious matters than embarrassing ourselves in front of a large crowd. Perhaps your job is on the line? This is still a case of perception. I can think of two examples.

The first happened back in the early 1990s. I was working for the Texas State Network, anchoring statewide newscasts. This was a pivotal point in my career. Glynda Chu was my news director. You'll remember I had impressed Glynda when we were both reporters in Austin. When she hired me, one of my duties at TSN was co-anchoring a noon newscast with Mary Peters. Mary was a loveable woman who would often make nervous gestures while we were in the anchor booth.

One day, she flubbed a line and made a face and a twitch that I found to be hilarious. I tried to remain professional and read the next line, but I couldn't get through it. I started laughing halfway through. The story was about a south Texas sheriff who had been killed in the line of duty. I was laughing about a gunned-down law officer! We quickly went to break.

After the newscast, Glynda called me into her office. Her phone was ringing off the hook. Radio stations across the state had heard the laughter and noted that we went to commercial break too early. Glynda told me that this was a fireable offense and could not happen again.

I was nearly in tears. What had I done? I went home thinking I was one mistake away from being fired. We certainly don't want things like this to happen, but there's a reason they have blooper reels at radio and television stations. The on-air talent does mess up from time to time.

Not only did I overcome this dark moment in my career, but I was able to advance to the national stage years later. Don't let one mistake set you back. And remember, the worst moment of your life may be a distant memory some day.

Ever do something and immediately wish you could take it back? You think to yourself, "If only I could do it over, I would have been more careful, or paid more attention." That happened to me long after I got my job at ABC News. I was working the overnight shift and was typing away, losing track of time.

I had already handed in my script for a sixty-second update on the Iraq war, so I was thinking ahead to the next newscast. Before I knew it, I saw the clock and realized I had about thirty seconds before this update was to air. I couldn't find my script. The editor hadn't placed it in the tray, as is protocol. I had no choice but to run into the studio without a script.

By the time I got there, I was out of breath and out of time. I started ad-libbing about ten seconds after the update was scheduled to air, positively rambling. It was horrible and there was no telling how many radio stations were counting on the update.

Lucky for me, most of them didn't wait around for ten seconds. They simply thought the network screwed up and there was no newscast. Timing is very precise when you work for a radio network. If you are even one or two seconds late, the local stations move on.

I felt like the wind had been knocked out of me. Not because I was out of breath from running, but because I had screwed up so royally. I didn't know what else to do, so I wrote an email to our vice president and my supervisor, letting them know what happened. I accepted full responsibility and told them it would never happen again.

My supervisor told me the email went a long way with the big boss, who appreciated my honesty and straightforwardness. I never missed another newscast and I spent many more years with ABC, hardly giving that one mistake a second thought.

The Ultimatum

Back in 1994, I was working at a news radio station in Dallas, Texas. A new program director had been hired. Michael Spears was a hotshot who was admired throughout the industry. Michael was one of those guys who colored his hair to keep the gray out. He was somewhat of a metrosexual before that word was even coined. He was a charismatic fellow who could charm people with his positive vocabulary and his big smile. I thought of him more as a used car salesman—there was something not quite authentic about the man.

That was my perception of him but I tell you now I was biased because of one five-minute meeting with the guy. I would see a different side of Michael the day he called me into his office and asked me to listen to a three-minute recording of our radio station that morning.

Michael said, "You're slowing the station down. Everyone else sounds full of energy and then you come on and drag us down." Then with a stern, I-don't-like-you-very-much-right-now look on his face, he said, "Fix it."

This was the worst day of my life, I remember thinking. I was devastated. My job was in jeopardy. I was so insecure that I took this very personally and from that point on I hated Michael Spears.

But being afraid I would lose my job, I put more energy into my voice during the very next newscast that day. Michael even popped his head into the booth and said, "That's the fastest I've ever seen anybody change. Good job." This is where the story should end happily ever after. Michael was happy, my job was safe, and all is well that ends well.

Not for me. I was still angry, offended, and full of self-doubt. My hatred of Michael would continue for some time. I was vindictive too. When Spears purchased a BMW convertible, I told a friend I wanted to take a crap on his front seats. All this anger because my boss told me to step it up a notch so that the radio station would sound cohesive.

Thankfully I never had the opportunity to defecate in Michael's sports car. Because of my new energetic news delivery, the program director of a brand-new station in Dallas called, asking if I was available. Indeed I was. I was hired across town to work for the competition. I took the job because it offered a boost in pay, but mainly I wanted to show Michael that I was valuable. I *was* good and an asset.

That job led to another, in New York City. For a broadcaster, and in many other career fields, New York is the cream of the crop—

the top rung on the ladder. It would be many years later before I realized the worst day of my life might have been one of the best.

Michael Spears did me a huge favor. My voice and inflection had been lagging. I was not energetic and it would have been hard for me to advance my career that way. By stepping up my game, I landed a new job. And the newfound confidence allowed me to grow even further, landing a prime spot in the Big Apple.

A lot of time and energy went into the negative feelings I harbored for my boss. Had I recognized what was happening, my world could have gotten a whole lot better a whole lot faster. Michael wanted the radio station to have an upbeat, big city sound. By asking me to step it up, he was giving me a gift that I was too naïve to recognize.

And what's worse is that I could have taken that advice and sought Michael out as a mentor. With all his years in the business, imagine the wealth of knowledge and the tips he could have given me to make me a better broadcaster! But I was too busy trying to show him that I didn't need his help and I wasn't inferior.

Don't get me wrong; this was actually a great motivator. But it also ate at me. Somewhere in my gut I knew he had a point. After more than a decade, I would realize that nothing Michael had said had been a personal attack. He had been helping me, making me a better newsman. Unfortunately Michael passed away before I was able to realize the gift he gave me. I would never get to thank him for advancing my career.

There is a second lesson here for anybody in a supervisory position, or those who aspire to be a manager. Be an inspiration to your employees. Don't rule by force. You may get what you want in the short run, but it will come back to hurt you in the long term.

Michael had an almost angry disposition when he told me to "fix it." I did because I feared what would happen if I didn't. But imagine if my boss had made me listen to that recording and then said, "Brad, you are a hard worker and it's appreciated, but I want to help you become a better broadcaster. Your delivery is too slow and here's what you can do to fix it."

Not only would Michael have achieved the results he wanted, but he would have boosted my ego, telling me he believed in my future and wanted to get me to a higher level. I would have been grateful and probably would have stayed with that radio station even when the competition came calling. There would have been a sense of loyalty that at the very least would have had me thinking long and hard before leaving. As it was, I accepted the job the minute they offered it.

We're always quick to identify a bad day, but we sometimes forget to look for the positive aspects of what may seem like a very negative situation. I don't want to imply that you can make any bad situation a positive one. Sometimes that's not the case. A medical diagnosis, death in the family, or some other lousy life event doesn't necessarily have an upside. So no need to try to make it something it clearly isn't.

Obviously, we deal with some things that are unfortunate and make us feel down for hours, or even days, but when you are having a bad day, take a step back and analyze the situation. You may in fact be having one of the best days of your life!

Lesson:

1. Life is arbitrary. There are no good or bad days. There are just days.
2. When times look bleak, remind yourself this could be a learning experience and lead to better opportunities ahead.
3. Be a motivator. People need reassurance in order to move forward. Be a positive influence rather than a negative one.

CHAPTER 9

Letting Go

A home, a steady job, a lasting marriage—people want permanence in their lives. We strive for it. We feel secure knowing
that something will remain stable in our lives without risk of change.
Maybe the bedtime stories our parents read to us when we were
children put this idea in our heads. We believe all stories end
"happily ever after."

Sarah, a friend of mine, called to tell me she had just gone
through a difficult breakup. It was all perfectly amicable. There was
no knockdown, drag-out fight. Quite simply, two mature adults
had decided after many months of dating that they weren't compatible. They would go their separate ways, but try to remain friends.

Sarah was finding this difficult because she still harbored feelings for the guy and found him wildly attractive. One of the issues
between them was that he would not give up part of his busy work
schedule to make more time for her. It was a continual bone of

contention. The question she had for me was, "How do you get over something like this?" That was followed by, "How much time will it take?"

My answer to Sarah was that *she* would decide how much time it would take. And getting over it? Just let go! When you are the son of a military man, you learn to do that very quickly and very early. When you move constantly all your life, you learn two things: nothing in life is permanent and you cherish the time you spend with people. We moved every few years for my entire childhood. That meant leaving friends behind at every air force base and then embarking on a new journey at the next military installation.

When I was in fifth grade, we lived in Charleston, South Carolina. My best friend then was Davey Angland. He was a couple of years older than me, but we both shared a love for Matchbox cars. We would trade them, shop together for new models, and even purchase model paint to give our cars new coats.

Davey and I were pretty much inseparable. I loved eating lunch at his house. His mother introduced me to kosher dill spear pickles and I fell in love instantly with their sharp tanginess. I'd always liked dill pickles, but there was something about the sliced kosher variety that excited my taste buds. They've remained a favorite snack, and I keep at least a jar or two in my refrigerator at all times.

When the time came to move, Davey and I said our goodbyes and promised to keep in touch. We didn't have Facebook or even email back in the 1970s, so after writing a letter or two, we stopped communicating. But every time I bit into one of those pickles I would relive the great moments I shared with Davey, often wondering what he was doing at that moment.

The initial pain of leaving a friend would pass with time. We got used to this way of life, knowing we'd lose contact and meet a new set of friends at the next air force base. After we moved to Panama,

I met up with an old friend. Keith Turbeville was quite a character. His father, like mine, was in the air force, and both men had been stationed in South Carolina just a few years before the two families moved to Panama.

Keith and I became fast friends and complemented each other well. I was the reasonable one who kept Keith grounded. He was more daring, always challenging me to do crazy things. Participating in our own war games, we slashed paths through the Panamanian jungle with our machetes and spied on classmates at school. Every day, Keith would walk into the nurse's office, grab her clipboard, and examine it studiously as if he were a doctor. "What are we seeing today?" he would ask her before she could grab the clipboard back in apparent disgust. Secretly, I think she was amused by his outrageous behavior.

It was Keith's mother who introduced me to the officers' club. My dad was a non-commissioned officer (remember the have-nots?) while Keith's family represented the upper echelon. One day, we all went to lunch together and had tacos in the officers' club. I was tremendously impressed. This was an exclusive club and I felt like a voyeur, seeing something I wasn't supposed to be viewing. Except that I wasn't on the outside looking in that day. I was on the inside, part of the elite crowd.

I remember the feeling of wanting to be "somebody," like an officer in the military. I wanted to be one of the "haves." I didn't want to be one of the less fortunate. I liked the feeling of being treated as if I were special. But all too soon I was forced to say goodbye to Keith when his father transferred to another base.

I was distraught. I'd already lost my friend, Davey, in our earlier move. Now I'd lost Keith. I took each separation with friends especially hard. During my teenage years, all my friends moved away. I was the only one left, and we still had nearly a year remaining before we would get our new assignment for another tour of duty.

I was so upset that my dad made me a "reverse calendar." This allowed me to count down the days until we left Panama for a new base, which meant new opportunities to make new friends. It was a huge help in getting me through those final, lonely months.

Keith and I wrote a few letters to each other and exchanged Christmas cards, but soon we faded apart, just like all my other friends. In those days before email or Facebook, a letter via snail mail was it. And teenage boys were not much interested in writing letters.

There was a part of me that felt I was going through the world alone. Sure, I had my family, and I would eventually make new friends, but there were periods where I was completely alone. With my chums coming in and out of my life, I knew nothing was guaranteed forever, which was a scary proposition for a shy teenager.

Over the years I would meet new friends and have a ton of fun laughing and playing, but then I'd always have to say goodbye. I guess the farewells became easier as time wore on, but they were always tinged with sadness. Leaving friends was never easy, but I did learn a lesson that I carry with me to this day: that as time passes, the pain of separation eventually subsides.

This was helpful in building my career. I never thought about the people I was leaving behind in order to take a new job in a different city. To me, it was all part of the routine. I was forty-four years old before I realized friends *should* be a consideration in any geographical move.

A close friend told me that when he left Alabama, he did not discuss it with his friends. When he planned a return visit to Birmingham, he expressed some concern about how his friends would react to his having left abruptly and without consultation.

This was the first time I'd ever considered the notion that friends might feel slighted if you just up and left. But why wouldn't they? They've spent time, as have you, building a friendship they thought would last, only to find you're on the next plane out of town.

I remember leaving my job in Waco, Texas, in the late 1990s. I'd made some great friends there and cried the day I left town. I really didn't want to leave them, but in my mind I had no choice if I was to advance my career. And since my job was my life, I packed up and left, tissues in tow to wipe away the tears. As time had proven in the past, I would recover and make new friends. And time has healed these wounds.

Friends can be temporary whether we part ways because of a job, grow apart, or have a falling-out. We must cherish the time we have with them. Letting go is a decision we can make for ourselves. If we need to end an abusive relationship, it may not be easy, but over time the hurt and pain will subside.

In my thirties, I anchored the nightly news in Oklahoma City for a few years. I loved that place. I had some wonderful friends and I was doing the very thing I was passionate about. It didn't hurt that my ego was being constantly fed by appearing on television and getting recognized in public. While furniture shopping one day, a family was winding its way through the store when the father stopped to say he watched me on television. We exchanged pleasantries and I was on cloud nine! To top it all off, I was driving a Mercedes. As a car fanatic, this was icing on the cake. I was at the top. I was in heaven. I thought it couldn't get much better than this.

And then ABC News in New York came calling.

Taking the job they offered me was a no-brainer. I'd get to live in New York City for a second time and I vowed that this time I would go out and really experience the city, which I hadn't done during my first stint in the Big Apple. During my early days at ABC,

I questioned whether I'd made the right move. Would it have been better to stay in Oklahoma? I'd had the job and friends I desired, but I had given up the balance of social and professional life just to climb the career ladder.

Certainly I missed my friends and my old life, but I was exploring New York and meeting new friends. And I was able to do some things that I couldn't afford to do back in the Plains. I was able to take some fantastic vacations. I was able to enjoy some time in the casino without worrying whether I would have enough to pay my bills. I was even able to purchase a new Porsche, the gold standard for automobiles. And perhaps more importantly, I met some wonderful people, not only in New York but also at my next stop, Los Angeles.

One locale led to another, and it was in L.A. that I met Richard Walther, who would become one of my closest friends and help me continue my transformational journey. Had I stayed in Oklahoma, where I wanted things to be permanent, my life would have been good. But I would have missed out on meeting some wonderful people who eventually became my closest pals. And I would never have found my way to The Landmark Forum, the venue that transformed my life, bringing me fulfillment each and every day. Change may seem scary. It may not even be what we want at the time. But life has a way of working itself out.

Let Go for the Sake of Others

One of my great heroes was my grandfather. Alfred Wagner was a big, barrel-chested man of German descent. He was an avid gun collector who owned a gun shop, car lot, convenience store, and gas station. He also had a campground that sat on a hilltop behind his gas station. I spent quite a few summers with Gramps and always had a great time. I would stand on the back of his tractor and wrap my arms around his big body as he mowed the grass in the campground. Occasionally he would drive us farther down the hillside for a hair-raising ride on the tractor.

During those hot summers I pumped gas and stocked the soda machines and beer coolers in the store. I felt like a man—a grown-up. I was ten years old and having the time of my life. At the end of the night we would lock up and reflect how business had been that day. I felt almost as if we were partners.

Grandma Florence would have something waiting for us to eat when we walked across the parking lot to the trailer where they lived. Gramps wanted to be on the same property to make sure nobody broke in and robbed the place. Whenever he heard a car pull up during the night, he'd jump out of bed, grab his rifle, and fling open the door. "Get moving, you son of a bitch!" he would snarl. Those who had pulled in to relieve themselves on the side of the building were taken by surprise.

Sometimes Gramps pulled the trigger, firing a warning shot toward the clifftop behind the store. I've never seen people move faster as they jumped in their car and sped away. I thought it was cool. In the entire time Gramps was in business, every station along a ten-mile stretch of highway had been robbed. Except one. His.

But Grandpa Alfred had a dark shadow dogging him. His brother, Howard, had died in World War II and had never been brought back to the States for burial. The year he died, their mother decided not to put up a Christmas tree—not that year nor any year after that. And Grandpa carried on that tradition.

I remember that as a child, whenever we visited during the holi-days, there was almost never a Christmas tree in my grandparents' trailer. Maybe a couple of years, here and there, my grandma managed to erect a small tree, but Alfred didn't like it and wasn't happy. My grandfather was honoring his dead brother. It was an honorable thing to do. Or was it?

The truth of the matter was that Uncle Howard was dead and would never return home. But my grandfather had forgotten about the people who were living, especially his grandchildren who believed in the magic of Christmas, which included a tree with all its trimmings. We missed out on some wonderful holiday memories because of it. It wasn't just the tree; Gramps was not a pleasant person to be around over the holidays. He couldn't let go. And it affected his life and those around him.

Mourning a lost relative is important, and those feelings can be raw. But eventually you have to let go and join the living. Otherwise you become one of the walking dead. The lesson here is that it's okay to let go. Grandpa could have let go, cherishing the memory of the sacrifice made by his brother, while knowing his grandchildren would get to spend a joyful holiday with the man they adored.

> Like the planet on which we live, we're always evolving, changing, and growing. Once we accept that, we can enjoy every moment and look forward to even greater ones ahead.

Similarly, leaving one job behind can lead to new opportunities in the future. And parting ways with friends doesn't always have to be a negative experience. We can cherish the memories we make together. It's human nature to want a sense of permanence in our lives. We want to know that we're safe and secure. Whether it be a job, a house, or a relationship, we want it forever.

But life, the world, is ever changing. Nothing in life is permanent. And that can be a good thing. Like the planet on which we live, we're always evolving, changing, and growing. Once we accept that, we can enjoy every moment and look forward to even greater ones ahead.

The Importance of Forgiveness

Part of letting go comes in the form of forgiveness. Many times we hold on to anger, and if we don't make peace with the person who did us wrong, it can consume our lives and prevent us from moving forward. Forgiveness means dropping our expectation of a certain outcome in life. You expect a friend to behave one way, but he does not.

Let's take Celia, for example. When she was a teenager, Celia's mother told her that she was not developing properly and her breasts were too small. "The boys aren't going to like a girl who's that small," her mother told her. Celia was devastated and resented her mother. During her adult years, Celia had breast enlargement surgery because she felt she wasn't big enough. She believed what her mother told her to be true.

When I questioned Celia about this, she said, "My mother claims she did her best. Well, her best wasn't good enough." Celia isn't about to forgive her mother for a problem that has haunted her all these years. She argues that any person with reasonable intelligence should know better than to tell a child this. You may find yourself agreeing with Celia. This is not a great example of parenting. So then, why should Celia forgive her mother? Mainly because their relationship is nearly nonexistent and this is still eating her up. If Celia can forgive her mother, she can move on. Perhaps they can have some sort of mother/daughter relationship, perhaps not. But they can both move forward and get on with life.

The first step in forgiveness is giving up the expectation of an outcome. Celia expected her mother to love her unconditionally and not point out her perceived flaws. We expect everybody to see the world as we see it, but that's not always the case, as I'm pointing out in this example.

Secondly, Celia needs to forgive herself for having such high expectations of her mother. Celia's mother is human, and we all make unwise decisions from time to time. When we screw up or make a bad decision, don't we want to be forgiven?

In Celia's case, placing the blame on her mother allows for justification of the breast enlargement and other aesthetic procedures she's had done over the years. Celia claims she was essentially forced to have the surgeries because of this idea planted in her head by her mother. By redirecting the blame, we can avoid responsibility. When the other person is always at fault, we have a scapegoat for our own actions.

It's easy to justify our unwillingness to forgive. Celia's mother was cruel, we say. She should have known better and has caused her daughter great pain over many years. But forgiving sets us free. When we forgive, the issue or the person no longer consumes us. We're able to move forward and evolve, rather than stay mired in negative thought.

Those who find it most difficult to forgive are often perfectionists, and the proof lies in the very fact that they won't let the other person off the hook. They believe the other person should be perfect, never making a mistake. These folks are terrified by their own perceived imperfections, and by focusing on another's "mistake," they don't have to look at their own faults or shortcomings.

Remember my friend Keith Turbeville from earlier in the chapter? He is now an ordained Episcopal priest. Keith says, "When we start to forgive, we can start to heal. When we share the gift of forgiveness toward others, not only can it help the other person, but we are truly the ones who benefit. Forgiveness can give us the peace that God truly desires for our lives so that we can be in close relationships with God."

No matter your religious affiliation or personal belief system, it is important to forgive. As humans we should be evolving, and when we don't make forgiveness a priority, we remain locked in our pasts, preventing us from growing. There is also great relief when you forgive. You free yourself from the bondage of holding a grudge. If there's a person in your life who has done you wrong, try to make amends. Start the process of forgiveness. You don't have to forget what this person has done, but you can forgive and get on with your life.

Choosing Friends

A great friendship can be very rewarding. And we must remember that we get to *choose* our friends. I often lost sight of that at various times in my life.

When introduced to someone, we get to assess whether they are a good fit for us. Over time, you discover more about that person and may realize he or she doesn't add to the quality of your life. Sometimes we have to let the person go. I also want to caution you that friendship is not a "one size fits all." There are varying degrees and definitions of friendship. Your idea of friendship may not mirror that of your new friend's. That doesn't mean you have to go your separate ways. If this person makes you feel good and adds to your quality of life, you may want to keep him or her around.

I have a group of friends in Los Angeles. We all get together occasionally and sometimes two or three of us socialize outside of the group. The guys vary in age, personality, and what they bring to the table. So my definition of friendship is different for each guy. One is my best friend. Our expectations of each other are different than that of other members of the group. So while I may expect my best friend to be there when I need to talk or to send a text wishing me the best on my first day of a new job, I don't expect that from some of the other guys.

Here's another example of varying definitions of friendship. If a friend needed my services—perhaps narrating a short film—I would be inclined to do the job for free. I'd consider it a favor since it wouldn't require much time and would help out my friend's budget. However, my friend may be a car salesman and when selling me an automobile, may decide to take his commission rather than rolling that into a discount for me.

Here's where it gets tricky. In the past, I would have been offended. "I narrated the short film for you and now you're going to take a commission off my sale?" I might have said. But now I know that my definition of friendship is giving of my services. That is not my friend's definition. However, we have a similar philosophy about life, we are great traveling companions, and we share a compatible sense of humor. These are great reasons to keep the friendship intact and continue building upon the foundation.

If the friend needs something in the future, I'm inclined to offer my services free of charge again, knowing that the favor might not be returned. That's okay. I'm still living within my definition of friendship, but allowing him to do the same. My way isn't necessarily the right way, nor is his. We need friends for support, socializing, and overall good mental health. When a friend is abusive, too negative, or does not enrich your life, it's best to part ways.

Many years ago, I moved to New York City. I didn't know a soul. A colleague of mine in Texas put me in touch with a woman named Cathy. A bit older than me, she was determined to find Mister Right. We shared a common bond: we were both journalists. Cathy showed me around the city, helping me get the lay of the land. We had many great conversations among our many adventures in the Big Apple.

On more than one occasion, Cathy asked to borrow money, a few hundred dollars at a time. She offered to write me a post-dated check and I obliged. Keep in mind that Cathy made a good salary; she just had a bit of a problem handling money and often fell short just before payday.

While many people think of New York as cutting edge, housing can be a much different story. Many buildings are old and have not been updated. It's quite common for buildings to be heated by steam. A giant water tank would percolate and send scorching hot water through the pipes of the building and into radiators inside each apartment unit. Central air conditioning is only common to newer, more modern buildings in the city. Apartments either have a unit just below the window (think of the kind of air provided in a motel) or tenants would install a window unit just before summer.

As a rule, I would install two window units in Cathy's apartment before summer hit and I would be asked to remove them and put them in storage at the end of the season. This was not an easy task as I was a thin guy, lacking muscles. But I knew it was an even tougher task for a woman in her fifties so I was happy to help out.

Cathy ended up losing her job—a devastating emotional blow to her. She was given six months' severance, so financially she had time to look for another job without worrying about the bills. Cathy decided to take some time off, visit friends out of state, and take a trip to Europe. I didn't blame her. Sometimes you need to take a break from it all, and being in between jobs is a perfect time to do it.

But my friend did not manage her money well. And before you know it, six months had gone by and she had not searched for another job. One day I got an email from Cathy, asking me if she could borrow rent money. The rent, more than a thousand dollars, had been due three days earlier. I wondered why Cathy would wait to ask me for the money. I simply wrote back that I couldn't lend her the money at this time. I didn't offer an explanation but did add that I would be willing to help her out with groceries.

Shortly after the email exchange, Cathy called me, almost in tears, saying she questioned our friendship. Did I not care about her? Why wouldn't I loan her the money? She knew I had the cash. I told her that I was concerned and did care, but couldn't offer a loan at this time.

Cathy told me I wasn't being a good friend. I explained how I had loaned her money in the past and how I changed out the air conditioning units year after year, among other favors. In my mind, I was a great friend. She didn't see it that way and after extensive arguing, I told her we needed to part ways.

As a practical matter, I thought to myself, "How would Cathy repay me the money?" Had I given her cash, she could have stayed in her apartment one more month. Even if she had gained employment, there would be weeks before the first check and she'd need that for the next month's rent and bills. I wasn't likely to get my money back for some time. And I had other friends and family members who also needed some financial help. Was I to ignore them? Cathy didn't appreciate what I had done for her over the years. She was scared and needed immediate cash. She was willing to give up a friendship when she didn't get what she wanted.

I had been generous and believe I'm still a giving person. But we all have our limits. Sometimes we just have to let the person go and fire our friends.

Lesson:

1. Letting go is a part of life. Friends may come and go and that can be okay.
2. Think long and hard before letting someone go. It may be wise, but you may also regret it.
3. Forgiveness is essential in moving forward with your life. Start to forgive and feel the weight of the world lifted off your shoulders.

CHAPTER 10

And Finally

We've gone over some good lessons for getting you started on your life's next journey . . . moving ahead and evolving . . . enjoying your life to its fullest. We should be ever changing—meaning that, in many ways, the person you were five years ago was different from the one you are now.

So where do you start? You begin with a vision. Who do you want to be and what do you want your life to be like a year from now? How about five years from now? Think about all aspects of your life. Where will you live? Will you be married? Will there be kids? What will you drive? What will your average day be like? Start answering these questions and you'll soon have a vision.

Some people want to make this a monumental task, but it's really easy. Do you daydream? Next time you do, take note of that respite from your day. There may be some answers in those daydreams.

I was living in New York in 2006 and thought I had convinced my bosses to allow me to do my job in Los Angeles, but the plan fell through. That didn't stop me from daydreaming and creating a vision of what I wanted.

On a daily basis, I'd picture myself getting into my Porsche and leaving the studio lot where our news bureau was located. I didn't even own such a fancy car. I also envisioned myself having dinner with friends at a great LA outdoor restaurant. I only knew one person in the city at the time and he wasn't really a good friend of mine. I thought about what it would be like to own a condo in Los Angeles and even pictured myself doing mundane chores like grocery shopping. Two years later, I was transferred to LA and found myself leaving the studio every night in my brand-new Porsche! I never gave up on that vision and it ended up paying off.

So many people consider themselves nearsighted when it comes to goals and their personal vision. They're not sure they can see the final result off in the distance. But I believe they are actually farsighted. The vision is clear—it's a dream that they'd like to turn into reality. But they just don't know how, or they believe it's so far-fetched they'll never get there.

I can relate. When I set out to write this book, I thought it would take me about six months to complete. I had ideas and all I needed to do was write them down and tell a story and I'd have my book. What I failed to realize at the time is that writing is time consuming and the passion is not always present. Sometimes there's writer's block. Some of the very ideas I had written down never made it into the book. They weren't important enough when it came down to choosing what made the cut and what didn't. This book has been more than three years in the making. I had to write it, my agent had to sell it to a publisher, and then the editing process, not to mention a delay or two in publication dates. Had someone told me at the beginning this would likely be a multi-year project, I might have been overwhelmed and dropped the whole idea. The thought of something taking three years seems like a lifetime, yet it can go by very quickly. I simply wrote when I felt inspired. My editor would go through my copy and send it back for a rewrite. Each day I felt inspired, I would write until the thoughts stopped flowing. I wasn't paying much attention to how many chapters I had written but rather the job at hand, cranking out material. It wasn't long before my editor printed out the manuscript and handed it to me one day. I couldn't believe it! I had actually written an entire book.

The idea is to create a vision and then start taking steps to achieve the goals along the way. Just do what needs to be done today and do it again tomorrow and then the next day, and the final vision will become closer. Because the dream seems so far away, we sometimes procrastinate and even fail to start toward a goal because it's overwhelming. If you want to lose weight, for example, you can set a vision and goals but what you really need to do is watch your intake right now—today! If you do that day after day and lose one pound a week, you'll have lost over fifty pounds in a year. If I told you it was possible to lose fifty pounds but it would take a year, you might give up before you even started. We want instant results, but success takes longer. People looking to earn a college degree might be intimidated by the number of classes required to secure a bachelor's, but one by one you mark off those credits and before you know it, four years have passed and you're walking across the stage receiving your diploma.

It is extremely important to start right now. "Act now, do not delay," as those TV ads so often say. By doing something each day, you get closer to what you really desire. Do something that you weren't doing yesterday, even if it doesn't fit into your vision. It may bring forth ideas or revelations that can help you achieve your goals.

Vision vs. Goals

Don't mistake goals for a vision. This is important—critical even—to your success. A vision is the broad picture—it's where you want to be in all aspects of your life. Goals are the stepping-stones to achieving that vision.

Let's say you want to lose weight. That's a "goal" many people set for themselves. If you set the goal to lose thirty pounds in six months, you are locked in with no wiggle room. In order to lose the thirty pounds, you'd need to drop five pounds each month. If this was just a goal and you missed the mark one month, you'd feel bad. Miss that mark a second month in a row and you'd feel like a failure. But if you create a vision for weight loss, you'll likely have more success and not suffer such great setbacks.

The vision is how your life will be different once you achieve the desired weight. How will your clothes fit? Will you be dating? Will daily walks be a part of your life? Will you be entertaining more? Will you opt for healthier foods? The list can go on and on.

Your thirty-pound goal can be a part of this vision if you like. But there will be other goals, such as getting some cardio three times a week or eating more vegetables. So if you miss that five-pound mark in a given month it's not such a big problem because your vision remains intact. This allows you to get back to the diet rather than feeling like a failure, plopping down on the sofa, and eating a quart of Ben & Jerry's.

A vision board may be a good way to begin your journey. It's simple. You can take a poster board and write down the things you wish to achieve. You can also cut pictures from magazines and glue them to the board. This could include a house, a car, a physique, a symbol of peace, etc. The vision board will give you something to look at every day and if you fail to reach a particular goal, you will still have the vision and can pick up right where you left off.

You Can Do It!

Once you have a vision and some goals, it's time to get out there and take action, and that can be very scary. We all experience fear and it's not a bad thing, unless it becomes paralyzing. Are you afraid you will fail to reach your goal? That too, is natural.

I've dealt with my share of fear applying for jobs or going on interviews. I had a pep talk that I would say to myself in the bathroom mirror, which helped me face the fear and go for it. Another way to get past the fear is to realize you are capable of whatever it is you're setting out to do.

Similar to a vision board, an accomplishment board can be a helpful tool. Rather than pasting pictures of things you want to accomplish, write down things you've already tackled. And if you are about to say you haven't accomplished anything, think again . . . long and hard. I'm sure you can think of something. This might be perfect attendance in grade school or winning a trophy for a sport. I listed major triumphs, such as my job in network news, but I also listed the city I built out of LEGOs when I was a kid as well as my title as commander of my Law Enforcement Explorers group. Write it all down, even something you consider minor or insignificant. Perhaps you can ask a parent or a sibling what they consider to be your accomplishments?

Once you have some items on the board, you can start reviewing it and letting it sink in. We've all been successful in our lives; sometimes we just need to be reminded. If you've managed to reach these goals in the past, what's preventing you from future victories? Absolutely nothing! You can do it and you need to know that. An accomplishment board can help you regain confidence. Putting things in writing can be a very effective tool in building confidence, easing anxiety, and putting things in perspective.

A client recently noted he was concerned about an upcoming move. Paul's roommate moved away and his landlord was about to hike the rent, so he was looking for a new place. He confided in me that he was somewhat cautious because he didn't want to choose the wrong area of town that could make him dislike San Francisco— even though he had lived there for several years.

I thought this was a rather strange notion, but Paul said if he chose a place too far from work, it would add to his commute, meaning he would have to wake up earlier to leave for work earlier, which could affect his quality of life. He also worried about choosing a sketchy neighborhood that he might regret later. Then there was the prospect of a new roommate; what if they didn't get along? If any of these negatives were to happen, Paul thought he might fall out of love with the city.

These are all legitimate concerns, but not worth stressing over. Rather than a full poster board, I told Paul to get a sheet of paper and write a list of places he'd lived. Then I told him to make note of whether he enjoyed his time at each of the locations.

It turns out that Paul had resided in some great homes and had some wonderful experiences over the years. There were a couple of not-so-great apartments, but nothing too scary. Now Paul could see his record of choosing homes and roommates was pretty good. He could now think about the area of town he'd like to live in and what kind of roommate he'd like to have, but he didn't have to obsess over it.

Whatever it is you are trying to accomplish, write down your past experiences, whether it be on paper or on a poster board, and keep reminding yourself of your victories. You are capable of making sound decisions and achieving greatness again!

Transformation

Transformation sounds huge, perhaps overwhelming to some, but it's not really a difficult process. Think of it as simple math—addition and subtraction. When you decide you would like to be a certain kind of person, start acting that way. Do it long enough and it becomes habit and a part of who you are.

I once told a friend this: "Today is a brand new day. Yesterday doesn't dictate who you are. You get to decide who you want to be right now."

She responded by saying, "The 'who' is the question of my life right now."

The "who" is not a major life question. It's not some persona you create and then stick with that image every day for the rest of your life. You are not locked in. Every minute of your life is "right now." Ten minutes from right now you could decide to make a change. Ten years from now you could decide to change again. That's the beauty of *now*. Every moment of your life is an opportunity for change and that can be a great thing, so embrace it.

This is an ongoing process. You start adding qualities that you wish to possess and start subtracting those you don't want. When you decide you want to be a giving person, simply start giving. Want to be more patient? Start exercising patience. This doesn't mean you won't suffer a setback or two, but keep pushing forward. If you make decisions each morning about who you want to be that day, you'll notice within six months you have qualities you never knew existed. By doing this, you become the awesome image you had in mind.

But what about that vision of the person you want to become? The vision is more about what your life is going to be like. The transformation is about what *you* are going to be like. And that's a step-by-step process that should continue for the rest of your life. Remember the chapter about our desire for permanence? We humans tend to want that with regard to who we are. We see a fixed image that never changes. It's more comfortable this way—more stable. But life is about change and growth, or should be, and we should embrace our ability to constantly take inventory of ourselves and make the changes that will get us closer to fulfillment.

The Greatest Lesson

The most important lesson of all is to make decisions for yourself. It's your life and only you know what serves you best.

Having spent time with likeminded people who enjoy self-help and the transformative genre, I've seen these folks find a philosophy in a book or at a retreat and try to live it to the letter. In fact, at one seminar I attended, the presentation was really about individuals thinking for themselves. But at the end of the three-day seminar, the company tried to upsell the next level of classes to us.

My teammates were worried sick. How would they say no to these people who seem to have all the answers? They were so focused on the leaders of the seminar knowing how to get into our minds that they forgot the most important lesson: think for yourself. I noted that we could simply say no if we desired and didn't have to offer an explanation. "We get to decide what's best for us," I told the group. This concept had never crossed their minds.

In the book *The Four Agreements*, author Don Miguel Ruiz talks about being impeccable with your word. That means being upfront and honest with people and not speaking ill of others or yourself. When you make this a habit, you can then say no without feeling bad about it.

Finding a philosophy that works is a great thing, but make sure you leave some room to expand, change, transform even more as you see fit. Don't get locked into something and stop growing. This book is my story; what worked for me. I'm sure you will find much of it positive, relatable, and helpful, but you don't have to pattern your life *exactly* the way I lived mine. Take the advice that works for you, embrace it, and move forward with your transformation. If you find something elsewhere that can add to your search for fulfillment, go for it!

That's a Wrap

Well, here we are at the end of the book. My life has been a wonderful journey as I've learned some valuable lessons and made a remarkable transformation. I'm not done growing and evolving as I continue to live and learn. I hope this will be the case for you as well.

My ultimate goal was to help people who've been struggling to find their way and provide a road map for life. These principles worked for me and I believe they will help you navigate around the roadblocks and speed bumps of life. Perhaps this book will allow you to leave some of the baggage behind.

The man I am today is a far cry from that shy, skinny kid who thought of himself as a freak and less than worthy. I was living the Perception Myth, unable to see the real me.

Stop labeling yourself in negative ways. See the positive attributes you possess. Remember that you are significant. You matter. Stop comparing yourself to others. Create a vision for the life *you* desire and then run your own race. Tap into that inner greatness to find the skills and qualities that will get you to the next level.

When you decide you want a change, that you want better, nothing can stop you.